"Every week at *America* magazine, I wait with eager anticipation to see what John Martens is going to say about the gospel for the coming Sunday or feast day. And I am never, ever, disappointed. Firmly grounded in the latest Scripture scholarship, wonderfully practical, and beautifully written, his reflections always teach me something new. Martens is that rare scholar that can write well for the general audience and, even rarer, say something new."

> — James Martin, SJ
> Author of *Jesus: A Pilgrimage*

"John Martens not only is an excellent biblical scholar but he also has a pastor's soul. These weekly reflections help us get inside the Scriptures each Sunday in a way that is scholarly, accessible, and spiritually rich. He makes the Word of God alive in so many thoughtful ways. This volume is a perfect synthesis of heart and mind, a place I can go to learn about the biblical readings for each week, be touched by God, and grow spiritually. I enthusiastically recommend *The Word on the Street* for all Christians, from thoughtful high school and college students to lay adults of all ages, and even (and especially) to theologians. Each reflection has something for everyone."

> — Peter Feldmeier
> Murray/Bacik Endowed Professor of Catholic Studies
> University of Toledo

THE WORD ON THE STREET

Year C

Sunday Lectionary Reflections

JOHN W. MARTENS

LITURGICAL PRESS
Collegeville, Minnesota

www.litpress.org

Library of Congress Cataloging-in-Publication Data

Names: Martens, John W., 1960– author.
Title: The word on the street, Year C : Sunday lectionary reflections / John W.
    Martens.
Description: Collegeville, Minnesota : Liturgical Press, 2018. | Originally
    published: 2015.
Identifiers: LCCN 2017058901 (print) | LCCN 2018024693 (ebook) |
    ISBN 9780814649909 (ebook) | ISBN 9780814649657
Subjects: LCSH: Church year meditations. | Bible—Meditations. | Catholic
    Church—Prayers and devotions. | Catholic Church. Lectionary for Mass
    (U.S.). Year C.
Classification: LCC BX2170.C55 (ebook) | LCC BX2170.C55 M3425 2018 (print) |
    DDC 242/.3—dc23
LC record available at https://lccn.loc.gov/2018024693

contents

Preface

For those who read the Bible as the word of God, it is a properly daunting task to write on the Scripture. God's word has been given to us for our salvation, to allow us to order our lives properly and to grow in holiness, which is to grow to be more and more like God. As the apostle Paul urged the Thessalonians, "we ask and urge you in the Lord Jesus that, as you learned from us how you ought to live and to please God (as, in fact, you are doing), you should do so more and more" (1 Thess 4:1). That is, to grow in holiness is a continuing process and so, too, is reading and understanding the Bible. It is a task that is never finished, in which new insights and developments continue to emerge. To be able to speak authoritatively on the Scripture, therefore, ought not to be an act of hubris, but an act of humility, reflection, and prayer in which God is allowed to speak to us and direct us.

The writings you find here are the products of a weekly process in which I spent time thinking about and praying with the readings for each Sunday, and pondering the things of my life, both ordinary and extraordinary, as I constructed my columns for *America* magazine's The Word and then returned to them and revised each of them as I prepared this book. It is a humbling task not just because I am writing on Scripture, but because I am aware of how many people have read the columns and will read this book, hoping to gain spiritual guidance, sustenance, and inspiration, and how many great scholars have written the column for *America* magazine in the previous years and decades. But then one adds to this the fact that some of the greatest minds ever have been writing on Scripture throughout the ages, such as St. Jerome, St. Augustine, St. Thomas Aquinas . . . and it is enough to make you throw down your quill (or keyboard) and wonder what you have to add.

And at this point, Scripture comes to our aid once again. You realize that the Bible is written for every age and it needs to be heard anew by every person, and that task will fall on some of us in every era. Paul claimed that he was "the least of the apostles, unfit to be called an apostle, because I persecuted the church of God. But by the grace of God I am what I am, and his grace toward me has not been in vain" (1 Cor 15:9-10). I am not comparing myself to Paul, but I am suggesting that each of us has a call, which even when we feel unworthy of it, God gives us the ability to fulfill. Paul went on to say that "I worked harder than any of them—though it was not I, but the grace of God that is with me" (1 Cor 15:10). I cannot say that I worked harder than anyone, but I can say that these columns emerge from my long training in biblical studies, my desire to grasp God's word and my willingness to sit with the Bible, in Greek and Hebrew, and to deliberate over each word, in order to answer a call I was not certain I was capable of fulfilling. More and more, I realize it is God's grace that enables the hard work and the skills that I claim as my own.

It is here, too, where I must thank my colleagues at *America* magazine, especially James Martin, SJ, Matt Malone, SJ, Bob Collins, SJ, Tim Reidy, Kerry Weber, and many others, who persevered in order to give me the opportunity to write the column, and who continue to encourage me along the way and do the hard work of editing my columns every week. They have allowed me the freedom to write on Scripture in whatever context emerges for that week and have given me unfailing support of whatever path I have chosen. In the same way, I wish to thank my editors at Liturgical Press for giving me this opportunity and shepherding it from start to finish with such professional care.

I also must thank my parents, John and Gertrude Martens, for instilling in me a great love of Scripture, which was cemented in the Mennonite church in which I grew up and by a large extended family on both my mother's and father's sides of the family. I grew up in an environment thoroughly drenched in Scripture, which was not seen as a dead letter, but as a living word that had been enacted, for instance, in bringing my family from the horrors of Stalinist Soviet Union to the refugee camps of post–World War II Europe and then to Canada. They did not and do not see these events as accidental, but as signs of God's providence. This is how they continue to read and interpret the Bible. Real interpretation of Scripture takes place at the ground level, in how we live our lives, and no one has helped me shape my interpretation of Scripture more than my own family, Tabitha, Sam, and Jake, who have aided me not just to think and to write about the Bible, but have challenged me to live out the Scripture every day, at street level.

Finally, however, I wish to thank all of you, the readers, who have sent numerous e-mails and handwritten letters (yes, readers send handwritten letters in envelopes still!) to encourage and support me every week. It is for the readers that this book is titled *The Word on the Street*. It is not intended to indicate a kind of hip knowingness about the ways of the world, but to indicate that Scripture is intended to speak to us where we live, whether the street, the suburbs, refugee camps, the big city, or the farm, and to meet us in our daily lives. Wherever you are and whatever stage of life you are in, God has something to say to you through the word of God. I am thankful that I can participate in this work and thank God for allowing this opportunity to speak with you. I hope you enjoy reading this book as much as I have enjoyed writing it, and I hope that these columns enable you to encounter God, the source of all true joy, in Scripture and on the street, as you go about your lives ordinary and extraordinary, certain in the knowledge that God is with you.

John W. Martens

WaITING In Love

First Sunday of Advent

Readings: Jer 33:14-16; Ps 25:4-14;
1 Thess 3:12–4:2; Luke 21:25-36

*"May the Lord make you increase and abound in love
for one another and for all."* (1 Thess 3:12)

Advent is a time of waiting and preparing. Tom Petty sang that the waiting is the hardest part, but it is even more difficult to determine how to prepare and how to use one's time to best advantage. While Advent is a time of preparing to welcome Jesus at Christmas, a celebration of the incarnation, it is also a time of looking forward to the return of Jesus at the eschaton. The eschaton, or "end of time," appears in popular culture—in novels, video games, and movies that draw on apocalyptic themes—as a time of warfare, battle, and grim hopelessness. How do these dark themes aid our waiting and preparation for the coming of the Lord?

First, it is important to acknowledge that Jesus does warn in dramatic language about the coming of the end. "There will be signs in the sun, the moon, and the stars, and on the earth distress among nations confused by the roaring of the sea and the waves. People will faint from fear and foreboding of what is coming upon the world, for the powers of the heavens will be shaken." But however such mythic language is to be interpreted, and I would opt for a figurative reading of these images, the end is not primarily about destruction, unless we are talking about the destruction of evil.

The flip side of the destruction of evil, of course, is the establishment of God's rule, because "then they will see 'the Son of Man coming in a cloud' with power and great glory" and when these events occur, "stand up and raise your heads, because your redemption is drawing near." The end is not about hopelessness; it is about hope, seen in the mythic language of the apocalypse as the conquering of evil, both inwardly and outwardly.

1

Preparing for a battle at the end of time is not how we are to prepare for the end—note that these images of warfare have to do with God's eradication of evil, not human warfare. Guns and tanks are not the means by which we are to await and prepare for our redemption. The prophet Jeremiah speaks of the kingdom of God as a place where the Messiah "shall execute justice and righteousness in the land" and the land itself, saved and in safety, says Jeremiah, will have a new name: "The Lord is our righteousness."

We are to prepare for the kingdom of righteousness, Jesus instructs, by placing ourselves "on guard so that your hearts are not weighed down with dissipation and drunkenness and the worries of this life" and to "be alert at all times, praying that you may have the strength to escape all these things that will take place, and to stand before the Son of Man." Yet, this is still only one type of preparation, waiting with the right attitude and the right mindfulness.

Paul teaches that day-to-day life is taking this right attitude and mindfulness and applying it not to the far future, events that may not loom in our own lifetimes, but to the way in which we conduct ourselves in every action, small or large. Paul says, "we ask and urge you in the Lord Jesus that, as you learned from us how you ought to live and to please God (as, in fact, you are doing), you should do so more and more." It is not an accident that not long after these instructions for righteous living, which Paul acknowledges the Thessalonians have been carrying out, that he speaks of the coming end. The way to prepare for the end is to live our lives in a way pleasing to God.

Yet, we are not alone in our task and so not alone in waiting and preparation. In fact, Paul stresses that the basic tasks of the Christian life, to grow in love and holiness, are supported through God's grace active in our lives. Paul says, *"May the Lord make you increase and abound in love* for one another and for all" and *"may he so strengthen your hearts in holiness* that you may be blameless before our God and Father at the coming of our Lord Jesus with all his saints." The one we are awaiting and preparing to greet is the same one who even now is with us and aiding us in our preparations.

As you await the coming of Christ, how are you preparing for his return?

AnTICIPATION

"The Lord has done great things for us, and we rejoiced." (Ps 126:3)

To anticipate is to expect. And to expect great things from God is not to be disappointed. The promises of Scripture are breathtaking, shocking, defying common expectations, seeming not to be met, yet satisfying, even in the waiting. For what others cannot see externally, we know in our hearts, our minds, our souls has come, is coming, will come to pass. The psalmist expects restoration even in the midst of suffering: "May those who sow in tears reap with shouts of joy." It is on the basis of God's past faithfulness that the psalmist looks forward to God's final renewal.

Indeed the Old Testament as a whole anticipates healing and restoration. Baruch instructs the people of Israel with a beautiful image drawn from everyday life: "Take off the garment of your sorrow and affliction, O Jerusalem, and put on forever the beauty of the glory from God. Put on the robe of the righteousness that comes from God; put on your head the diadem of the glory of the Everlasting." Mourning garments, sackcloth torn and ripped in displays of sorrow, will be replaced by heavenly garments, everlasting displays of God's righteousness and reign.

Yet, Baruch's vision of the future is not just for those who read the words after return from exile, but for those still to return, the exiles of the Assyrian and Babylonian captivities, "your children gathered from west and east at the word of the Holy One." These words of Baruch, echoing the prophet Isaiah, foresee the coming of the kingdom built in the presence of all the tribes returned, but even more, a world made new—"for God has ordered that every high mountain and the everlasting hills be made low and the valleys filled up, to make level ground, so that Israel may walk safely in the glory of God."

It is the same prophet Isaiah that echoes once more in the mouth of John the Baptist, as the Gospel of Luke presents him crying out to those in Judea, "Prepare the way of the Lord, make his paths straight. Every valley shall be filled, and every mountain and hill shall be made low, and the crooked shall be made straight, and the rough ways made smooth; and all flesh shall see the salvation of God." Note the difference, however, in John's vision and that of Baruch: the future is built on the return of the exiles, as Baruch envisions, symbolized in Jesus' ministry by the twelve apostles, but in Luke it is a call of salvation that extends to all the nations of the world. As John the Baptist says, "all flesh shall see the salvation of God."

It is this very process, of awaiting and preparing for the coming of God's kingdom, inaugurated by the first coming of the Messiah, that emboldens and fires the work of the church, such as seen in the ministry of Paul and Timothy. The saints, the holy ones in Christ Jesus at Philippi and beyond, including the bishops and deacons, says Paul, are also engaged in work of cosmic significance. This work is to prepare one another and to bring others into the kingdom as we await the Parousia or coming of Christ.

This is not work, however, in which we struggle on our own, for we are supported by our brothers and sisters in Christ, laypeople and clergy, and most significantly supported by God. Paul tells the church he is "constantly praying with joy in every one of my prayers for all of you, because of your sharing in the gospel from the first day until now." He acknowledges his support and the work of the church. But Paul is also "confident of this, that the one who began a good work among you will bring it to completion by the day of Jesus Christ." It is not our own work, though we are key participants, helping and supporting one another, but the work of God. Paul's prayer for us is nothing but that our life be modeled on the divine life, for he prays "that your love may overflow more and more with knowledge and full insight to help you to determine what is best, so that in the day of Christ you may be pure and blameless." This is our work: to cooperate with God's work in us as we await the coming of the kingdom in fullness.

As you await the coming of Christ, how are you working to build the kingdom?

JOY AND GENTLENESS

Third Sunday of Advent

Readings: Zeph 3:14-18; Isa 12:2-6;
Phil 4:4-7; Luke 3:10-18

*"Let your gentleness be known to everyone.
The Lord is near."* (Phil 4:5)

Some people decry the loss of manliness today, the feminization of men, but manliness in this caricature is often a crude stereotype: men like cars, sports, and beer; they are tough guys who do not cry, have no time for social niceties, chick flicks, or emotion. They work with their hands, build things, and treat the confines of an office cubicle with horror. There are men like this, but it is problematic when masculinity is categorized as any one sort of character, such as stoic tough guy.

Why do we not, for instance, take images of masculinity from biblical figures, like Jesus or Paul? How do they live out their masculinity? Advent, a time of preparation, is also a time for reconsideration and reflection, a time to consider change, renewal, and restoration. Waiting can lead to conversion. Paul's letter to the church in Philippi offers opportunities for reflection on and conversion of a certain type of masculinity that desires always to be in power and control, though Paul's advice transcends gender and its stereotypes. Philippians is a letter focused on rejoicing no matter how difficult our conditions and circumstances; it is a letter about letting go and trusting in God's plan.

Paul is in prison as he writes to the Philippians, and he encourages them to "Rejoice in the Lord always; again I will say, Rejoice. Let your gentleness be known to everyone. The Lord is near." There are two admonitions that stand out here: the call to rejoice; and the call to gentleness. Paul is engaged in his own waiting while imprisoned, but he calls on his fellow Christians to rejoice whatever the circumstance and to "let your gentleness be known to everyone." The word Paul uses here for gentleness, *epieikes*, also has the sense of graciousness, forbearance, and civility, which is to be made known to "all people" (*pasin anthrôpois*). Waiting in difficult circumstances is hard enough, for anyone who has spent time in doctors' offices, car repair shops, or in line at government offices: nerves get jangled, tempers fray and break. Paul's advice comes as he awaits his possible execution.

No matter the circumstance, Paul instructs us that patient joy is required as a Christian. In some ways the Christian life as a whole is a life of waiting, not just for the advent of the Messiah but for holiness to grow and our vices to wither. We are called upon to wait and endure not just situations but people with gentleness, tinged with graciousness, forbearance, and civility. For those of us who wait on pins and needles, unease our constant companion, or on the verge of breaking down, with anger poking through our veneers of civility, this is advice that must be lived in little ways on a daily basis.

The ability to rejoice in God emerges from our willingness to treat small or large situations, and most significantly people, with gentleness. Indeed this is what allows us to experience joy in our lives. Moments in our lives transformed by the grace of God from near occasions to anger, venting, and cruelty to times of gentleness, restraint, and kindness.

This is, of course, advice from Paul on how to live out our Christian life for all people, men and women, but the focus on gentleness in Paul's guidance is often seen as a female trait. Paul's counsel, though, is in plural, "you as a whole," not for individuals, but for the whole church. However we live out our Christian lives, and the various gifts we have, our life must show constant evidence of joy and gentleness, especially as men who are used to imposing our wills on others, being in charge, and making our ways known. This is the challenge of waiting, of allowing it to transform us in holiness and create in us joy.

It is what we want most deeply. When the crowds went to see John the Baptist, thinking he might be the Messiah, but certainly awaiting the Messiah, for "the people were filled with expectation," they asked one question, over and over: "What then should we do?" John gave a variety of specific answers for people in general and for soldiers and tax collectors in particular. The answers in specific can indeed be multiplied, yet it must be said that in all of our preparations to welcome the Messiah joy and gentleness ought to be high on the list and these traits allowed to challenge common notions of masculinity.

As you await the coming of Christ, how are you expressing your joy and gentleness?

THE Prophetic Word

Fourth Sunday of Advent

Readings: Mic 5:1-4; Ps 80:2-19;
Heb 10:5-10; Luke 1:39-45

*"And blessed is she who believed that there would be a fulfillment of
what was spoken to her by the Lord."* (Luke 1:45)

At the heart of the biblical tradition is the understanding that the word
of God has been revealed and that this revelation is for our good, particularly our salvation. For Jews and Christians who read the Bible as the word
of God, there is tension between what the text meant in its original historical context, the literal sense, and to what the text denotes in our own
day and age. Some of this is simply trying to understand the literal sense
itself, but other interpretation has to do with understanding spiritual
senses, such as allegorical and typological, how they are related to the
literal sense, and how the prophetic word is fulfilled. Naturally, wondering how the prophetic word is fulfilled indicates a belief in the prophetic
nature of Scripture.

Micah, the eighth-century BCE prophet, who was active during the
Assyrian conquest of the northern kingdom, outlined the dire reality that
Israel was "walled around with a wall; siege is laid against us; with a rod
they strike the ruler of Israel upon the cheek," but still prophesied a future
king from Bethlehem. In the midst of the crushing defeat of Israel and the
profound threat to Judah, Micah spoke the word of the Lord, which Christians believe was fulfilled over seven hundred years later.

"But you, O Bethlehem of Ephrathah, who are one of the little clans of
Judah, from you shall come forth for me one who is to rule in Israel, whose
origin is from of old, from ancient days. Therefore he shall give them up
until the time when she who is in labor has brought forth; then the rest of
his kindred shall return to the people of Israel. And he shall stand and
feed his flock in the strength of the Lord, in the majesty of the name of the

Lord his God. And they shall live secure, for now he shall be great to the ends of the earth; and he shall be the one of peace."

This messianic prophecy was uttered at a time when the conditions for its fulfillment would have seemed foolish; encrypted in the prophecy are signs about a coming time of prosperity and eternality that belie the actual historical age in which it was given. There is the promise that the one who is to rule Israel has his origin "from of old, from ancient days," that the people "shall live secure," and that "he shall be great to the ends of the earth; and he shall be the one of peace." Why did Micah say such things that he would never live to see? Because the prophet's task is to speak the word of the Lord, whether favorable or unfavorable, whether for their time, as it most often was, or for a time still to come.

The prophetic word is not always or even usually that straightforward, and certainly the Jews of Jesus' day were divided on whether this particular prophecy had been fulfilled. Those Jews and Gentiles who were disciples of Jesus saw this as a prophecy fulfilled in Jesus' own birth in Bethlehem. Prophecy, indeed, understands that historical events bear out the activity of God in the world, even in the mundane activities of daily life. One could not categorize the birth of a child, any child, as a mundane event for those involved, especially not the mothers-to-be, their infant children, and the fathers and extended families, but birth is an everyday event, even if it was fraught with danger in the ancient world.

Mary's task in the fulfillment of the prophetic word was to hear the words of God and obey, to trust that the prophecy could be and would be fulfilled not only in her lifetime but in and through Mary herself. Part of this fulfillment was to meet with her relative Elizabeth, who was also miraculously pregnant according to Luke, and "when Elizabeth heard Mary's greeting, the child leaped in her womb. And Elizabeth was filled with the Holy Spirit and exclaimed with a loud cry, 'Blessed are you among women, and blessed is the fruit of your womb.'" Elizabeth ends her speech to Mary saying, "and blessed is she who believed that there would be a fulfillment of what was spoken to her by the Lord." And this itself is at the heart of the prophetic word: that we believe, regardless of circumstance, that there will be a fulfillment of what was spoken by the Lord.

Imagine yourself with Elizabeth, experiencing the presence of Jesus. What do you want to say to Mary?

THE ONLY SON, GOD

The Nativity of the Lord

Readings: Isa 52:7-10; Ps 98:1-6;
Heb 1:1-6; John 1:1-18

"He was in the beginning with God." (John 1:2)

The incarnation. It sounds rather systematic and theological to describe the birth of a baby. And it is. Every birth is a mystery, the enigma of creation transforming individuals, the family, and the world, but the birth of God in the world as a child? How else can one describe the mystery of God embodied in the person of the infant Jesus but to use technical terms? Yet, while this technical term describes the mystery, it cannot encompass the mystery or delight in the repercussions of the birth of the only Son, God.

The essence of God's ways are encapsulated by the birth of Jesus. Hebrews tells of God speaking to humanity "by a Son, whom he appointed heir of all things, through whom he also created the worlds. He is the reflection of God's glory and the exact imprint of God's very being, and he sustains all things by his powerful word." The Gospel of John tells of "the Word" who "was with God, and the Word was God. He was in the beginning with God. All things came into being through him, and without him not one thing came into being." Yet, this Son, the word of God, "became flesh and lived among us." Why did God take on flesh as an infant child and live among us? Why did God not choose some other way to reveal God's self to humanity?

It is important to know that God could have chosen some other way. St. Thomas Aquinas says that "it was not necessary for the reparation of human nature that God become incarnate, for God in his omnipotent power could have repaired human nature in many other ways" (*Summa Theologiae* [ST] III.1.2). God, for instance, could have taken on the form of a terrible warrior and destroyed all those who would not bow to the magnificent power; or God could have simply decided to forgive all sin and wipe it away. If Thomas is correct, as I believe he is, then the reason for

God choosing to restore humanity through the incarnation has to do with God's love of humanity. The incarnation was not necessarily the best way for God, but it was the best way for us.

Thomas believed that God became incarnate as human being, from infancy to adulthood, because it increased the good in us. In terms of the theological virtues, the incarnation increased our faith, hope, and love. There is no greater sign of God's love for us than that God took on human form, shared our nature, and lived among us. Even more than this, Thomas suggests that a human savior offers us a model to follow, God in the flesh, and that such a model allows us to see in the words of St. Augustine that "God was made a human being, that the human being might become God" (ST III.1.2).

St. Thomas Aquinas, though, also believed that the incarnation has a positive effect on removing evil. It is not evil that has taken on human nature, but God, which indicates "how great is the dignity of human nature, lest we defile it by sinning" (ST III.1.2). The incarnation also removes presumption of any individual because God's grace is given to all humanity not due to anyone's merits but because of God's coming among us. The incarnation, then, heals the pride of humanity through the humility of God and offers for our salvation a human person who is like us in every way but sin.

St. Anselm reflects in a similar way on the incarnation, focusing especially on the humility of God when he asks, "Why did you conceal such power under such humility?" Anselm proposes that God concealed power in humility not "to conceal what was known of yourself, but to reveal what was not known." And what God revealed in the humility of the incarnation was that "it was for the sake of human nature that all these things needed to be done, so that it might be restored to that for which it was made" (*Meditation of Human Redemption*, 34–44, 85–87). The incarnation, that is, was necessary so that human beings could become what we were intended to be. The birth of the only Son revealed to us Jesus' "glory, the glory as of a father's only son," but the intention was so that "all who received him, who believed in his name, he gave power to become children of God, who were born, not of blood or of the will of the flesh or of the will of man, but of God." God became a child so that we might become children of God.

Reflect on the incarnation. How does God's humility reveal God's glory to you?

THE FAMILY OF GOD

Readings: Sir 3:2-14; Ps 128:1-5;
Col 3:12-21; Luke 2:41-52

"After three days they found him in the temple." (Luke 2:46)

The notion of what constitutes a family rages in Western culture today, with various countries and states adopting an expansion of marriage to include same-sex relationships. Historically, in Judaism and Christianity, such relationships have not been deemed acceptable, let alone consecrated or called marriage, though the view of marriage seen throughout the Old Testament is more expansive than we might now consider, including polygamous marriages among the patriarchs and matriarchs. At the heart of the family, though, has always been the child, which throughout history until recent times required a mother and a father. It is not that parents did not die or divorce, leaving children orphaned, perhaps to be adopted, or to be raised by a single parent or extended family, only that there was no choice but to be traditional when the only way for a child to be born was through the union of a mother and a father.

The traditional structure of the family extended to the functions of the various household members. The Ten Commandments called upon children to honor their parents. Ben Sira builds on this commandment, stating that "those who honor their father atone for sins, and those who respect their mother are like those who lay up treasure. . . . Those who respect their father will have long life, and those who honor their mother obey the Lord." Ben Sira also calls upon the son in particular to "help your father in his old age, and do not grieve him as long as he lives; even if his mind fails, be patient with him; because you have all your faculties do not despise him." Built into the family were directions for caring for one another.

This same functional understanding of the family grounded the teaching of the author of Colossians, traditionally ascribed to the apostle Paul, in which, influenced by the Greco-Roman household codes, wives are called upon to "be subject to your husbands, as is fitting in the Lord," husbands to "love your wives and never treat them harshly," children to "obey your parents in everything, for this is your acceptable duty in the Lord," and fathers to "not provoke your children, or they may lose heart."

While anyone who has raised children is aware that discipline and order are required, and that honor of parents is required by the commandments, the more difficult issues come in the living out of family life: Of what does honor consist? What is proper discipline? What sort of honor is due to parents who are abusive to children? In the same way, the notion of subordination of men to women emerges from a social structure that saw women as unequal to men. What does it mean for a wife and husband who share parenting and work outside the home as equal partners to be subordinate to one another? These are important and necessary questions, for family life is often a messy affair, sometimes painful, though most often wonderful and the source of comfort.

What is also important is to recognize that families are families throughout time, usually not perfect, and prone to the daily distractions and problems of every family. But what is most essential is to acknowledge that every child, even the adult children who now serve as parents, are all children of God, whose existence relies upon God and not simply their human parents.

Jesus' family brings this to the fore in a special way. Jesus was brought forth in a unique manner, utterly unlike even the miraculous births that dot the Old Testament, but he lived with a mother and an adoptive father. It was a normal family, though Jesus did not live with two biological parents. And, though sinless, as we all imagine our own children to be as they sleep blissfully, Jesus behaved like a normal child, causing his parents to panic as they sought for him after the Passover festival, a miscommunication causing him to be left behind. "Child, why have you treated us like this? Your father and I have been looking for you with great anxiety." Where was he? "Did you not know that I must be in my Father's house?" His answer has a particular meaning for him as the Son of God, but really, whatever our family arrangement here on earth, however traditional it might be, we are all after all children of God, yearning for our true home.

How do you understand yourself as a child of God?

ADOPTED INTO THE FAMILY

Second Sunday after Christmas

Readings: Jer 31:7-14; Ps 147:12-20;
Eph 1:3-14; John 1:10-18

*"He destined us for adoption as his children
through Jesus Christ."* (Eph 1:5)

The central claims of the prologue in the Gospel of John are that the Word is God and that the Word became flesh and dwelled among us, but sometimes overlooked is the powerful claim that the followers of Jesus, those "who received him, who believed in his name," were given "power to become children of God, who were born, not of blood or of the will of the flesh or of the will of man, but of God." The incarnation has as its goal not simply the revelation of God, but the salvation of human beings as a part of God's one family.

This "one, big happy family" motif might sound like the aim of a sappy 1960s sitcom, but such a goal was imagined in nascent form long ago by the prophets. The prophet Jeremiah has the Lord speak of the gathering of the exiles of all Israel, including those tribes long ago lost in the Assyrian devastation. God speaks, saying, "See, I am going to bring them from the land of the north, and gather them from the farthest parts of the earth, among them the blind and the lame, those with child and those in labor, together; a great company, they shall return here. With weeping they shall come, and with consolations I will lead them back, I will let them walk by brooks of water, in a straight path in which they shall not stumble; for I have become a father to Israel, and Ephraim is my firstborn." At the heart of the ingathering is the notion that the whole family must be brought together for the family to be whole. In this language God is designated as "father" and the people as "my firstborn."

While this accounts for the people of Israel, what of the other nations? How are they to come to be a part of God's family, children of God? The author of Ephesians, traditionally thought to be Paul, says that God "destined us for adoption as his children through Jesus Christ" and that "in Christ we have also obtained an inheritance, having been destined according to the purpose of him who accomplishes all things according to his counsel and will." This focus on "children" and "inheritance" speaks of family belonging, naturally, and the claim that God "destined us for adoption" indicates that our inclusion in the family was always a part of God's plan.

Indeed, later in Ephesians, Gentiles are told that they were once, apart from Christ, "aliens from the commonwealth of Israel, and strangers to the covenants of promise, having no hope and without God in the world" (2:12), but that "in his flesh he has made both groups into one and has broken down the dividing wall, that is, the hostility between us . . . that he might create in himself one new humanity in place of the two, thus making peace, and might reconcile both groups to God in one body through the cross . . . for through him both of us have access in one Spirit to the Father. So then you are no longer strangers and aliens, but you are citizens with the saints and also members of the household of God" (2:14-19). Christ's task was to bring all the nations into a relationship with the Father by allowing us to be welcomed and adopted into the one family. Ephesians describes this family as "one new humanity."

The plan to create one family in God appeals to us not because of sentimentality but because sentimentality reflects God's destiny for humanity, which we recognize as a deep truth of human existence. God's purpose for humanity is indeed to recognize that we ought to consider one another brothers and sisters, adopted children of God through the Son. This is why even though many fight against the oneness of humanity, violently attacking others in the name of God or no God, or reject the notion that humanity could be intended to be one family, there is a visceral knowledge that offenses against this oneness are products of human sin. Racism offends deep human sensibilities as well as the plans of God. The torment of Ferguson, Missouri, is the torment of humanity in the sins that offend the plans of God for all of us. Those, like ISIS, who barbarically slaughter others because of different beliefs and practices do violence not just to the children of God but to the will of God, the Father, who desires not just that his church be one but that all people be welcomed at the family table.

Reflect on the notion of yourself as a daughter or son in God. How can you welcome others into the family?

THEOTOKOS

The Blessed Virgin Mary, Mother of God

Readings: Num 6:22-27; Ps 8:1-9;
Gal 4:4-7; Luke 2:16-21

"God sent his Son, born of a woman." (Gal 4:4)

The name of God bore a weight in antiquity that might surprise moderns who often use words carelessly and thoughtlessly, using the names of God in vain or as everyday curses. God's name is holy and at the time Jesus was born many Jews considered it unacceptable to utter the Hebrew name for God. The name of God was not always written on the page, with substitute words or even dots sometimes being adopted in its place. The power of God's name is seen in Scripture, with Numbers speaking of the blessing of God as being the equivalent of putting "my name on the Israelites," while Psalm 8, after describing the majesty and glory of God, interjects "how majestic is your name in all the earth!" If the name of God is holy, something to be treated with reverence by those who carry it in their minds, on their lips, and in their hearts, how much holier is the person of God? To this question we should add, who could be worthy to carry the incarnate person of God to birth?

Luke tells a story not of majesty or glory, but of lowliness and humility: the child Jesus born in a manger to the woman Mary. This would not be a remarkable birth by ancient standards, as lowliness and humility were the lot of most human beings in antiquity and modern antiseptic conditions known to hospitals today unknown even to the high and mighty in Jesus' day. Indeed, the choice of the Creator of the world to be born as an infant was itself the choice of humility, wherever and whenever such a birth would have taken place.

The birth of Jesus, though, took place precisely when it was supposed to, for "when the fullness of time had come, God sent his Son, born of a woman, born under the law." For Jesus' birth hinged upon the preparedness of his mother Mary to accept the task of her own free will, carry her

15

holy infant to his birth, and then raise him according to the teachings and practices of the Torah, such as circumcising the boy Jesus on the eighth day in accordance with the law.

According to Luke, Mary, who was the favored one, or "full of grace," had been instructed in these things by the angel Gabriel. She knew that her son would be the savior of the world—even his name had been revealed by Gabriel—and at his birth when the shepherds revealed what they had seen and heard, "Mary treasured all these words and pondered them in her heart." Later Christian theologians would reflect on what it meant that Mary was chosen, what it meant that she was "full of grace," and still later, church leaders would name her Theotokos or "bearer of God," sometimes translated as Mother of God. The name Theotokos caused considerable discussion and dispute in the early church, for it is demonstrably the case that Mary did not bring God into creation, but how should the one who brought the incarnate Son of God into human existence be described? She carried the infant boy to his ordinary birth, but this only indicated her own remarkable human existence, especially prepared and chosen for this unique task.

Mary's holiness was essential to carry the holy second person of the Trinity, but her unique human holiness points to the holiness that is the destiny of human beings that God desires for all of us. Paul tells us that Jesus was born of a woman precisely "so that we might receive adoption as children." The kingdom of God needs to be peopled by those who choose God as their Father and who grow in holiness so that they can live in the presence of the Holy Trinity. God is preparing us for our destiny even now, "and because you are children, God has sent the Spirit of his Son into our hearts, crying, 'Abba! Father!' So you are no longer a slave but a child, and if a child then also an heir, through God." The kingdom is our inheritance and to prepare us for it note that God has sent "the Spirit of his Son into our hearts" carrying with it the name of God, "Abba! Father!" While Mary the Theotokos was alone fit to carry the Son of God, we must carry with holiness the name of God, allowing ourselves by grace to be transformed by his presence on our lips, in our hearts, and in our minds, in preparation to spend eternity with God.

Reflect on Mary carrying Jesus in her womb. How can you prepare yourself to carry the name of God into the world?

super star

Readings: Isa 60:1-6; Ps 72:1-13;
Eph 3:2-6; Matt 2:1-12

"Nations shall come to your light, and kings to the brightness of your dawn." (Isa 60:3)

Stars in antiquity were sometimes associated in pagan lands with divinities and even among the Jews they might represent the resurrected righteous, as in Daniel. They also, of course, played a major role in ancient astrology, whose practitioners believed the stars determined the sort of life a person was destined to live. While Jews and later Christians would reject the notion of astrology as indicating the life a person was predestined to live, the stars also played a role in antiquity in what we might call the science of astronomy. If the stars and the planets could not determine one's future, they could guide one's path. It can be difficult to imagine how bright the stars were in antiquity where the glory of the stars and the moon were not outshone and dimmed by innumerable artificial lights.

According to Matthew, the magi read the stars, for guidance on a physical and a spiritual journey, to find a newborn king. Isaiah's spiritual prophecy of the light and glory of the Lord dispersing the darkness that covers the earth, the "thick darkness" that shrouds the peoples, is interpreted by Matthew as both physically and spiritually fulfilled in the birth of Jesus. Isaiah writes that "nations shall come to your light, and kings to the brightness of your dawn," and that "they shall bring gold and frankincense, and shall proclaim the praise of the Lord." Matthew sees the magi as a symbol of the nations and, of course, the gold and frankincense among their physical gifts. Isaiah's vision, of course, is not just for the traveling magi, but for all people to recognize and respond to the light and glory of God. Isaiah foresees the people of the nations and instructs the reader to "lift up your eyes and look around; they all gather together, they come to you; your sons shall come from far away, and your daughters shall be carried on their nurses' arms."

This was the true promise of the Messiah, envisioned throughout the prophetic literature, that Israel's king would be recognized by the world when he came to establish peace. Given Israel's history as a conquered people, it was not a hope based upon their own physical might or military power, but in a God who cared for all people and all nations. The psalmist imagines, like Zechariah 9:10, that the king will "have dominion from sea to sea, and from the River to the ends of the earth." He was to be a king of righteousness and justice who cares for the weak and the needy.

Matthew sees these prophecies fulfilled in the lowly birth of Jesus in Bethlehem, for the magi "observed his star at its rising, and have come to pay him homage." When they find Jesus, through the guidance of the star, they do not draw back from the unroyal surroundings or poverty of the family, but they become "overwhelmed with joy." They pay Jesus homage, *proskynêô* in Greek, which denotes the worship of the king, and offer to "him gifts of gold, frankincense, and myrrh." Matthew's meditation on Jesus' birth offers us insight not only into ancient prophecy and fulfillment but the hopes of people in his own day and ours: we desperately seek the king who will rule with righteousness, and offer justice for the weak and needy.

In our own world we see the weak and the needy suffering, we see righteousness absent and justice often gone awry. It is not only our task to wait for the king to be revealed, but like the magi to seek him out, to seek where the star burns brightest. There will always be latter-day King Herods who seek to quash the search for peace and justice, who desire power over righteousness. In our daily search for the true King, Jesus, we must be vigilant and bring him the sorts of gifts that do him the greatest homage: those that make his kingdom present in this world and make the peace that he promises apparent for everyone. We wait with expectation, while we work for the establishment of God's kingdom.

As the author of Ephesians, traditionally understood to be the apostle Paul, says, "in former generations this mystery was not made known to humankind, as it has now been revealed to his holy apostles and prophets by the Spirit: that is, the Gentiles have become fellow-heirs, members of the same body, and sharers in the promise in Christ Jesus through the gospel." Our task is to seek out the King and build the kingdom for all.

Consider the epiphany of Christ. How can you best make known his kingship today?

SON OF GOD

The Baptism of the Lord

Readings: Isa 42:1-7; Ps 29:1-10;
Acts 10:34-38; Luke 3:15-22

"You are my Son, the beloved; with you I am well pleased." (Luke 3:22)

In discussions with Muslim theologians from Dokuz-Eylul University and Christian theologians from the University of St. Thomas, I presented the New Testament portrait of Jesus as both God and Man, a concept that they found confusing and unconvincing. My explanation centered on a specific reality to which the texts bore witness: this was how the first followers had experienced Jesus, in ways that would shatter their own understanding of Jewish monotheism. Current discussions that try to unravel the systematic and logical ways in which we can speak of Jesus as both human and divine—though a necessary task of theology and philosophy—often are founded on the simple reality that the first disciples of Jesus were passing on what they had seen and lived, not what they had formally defined and logically upheld in creedal statements.

The Gospel of Luke tells us that the people were expectant, wondering if John the Baptist might be the awaited Messiah; but John explained that he was not the Messiah and continued his ministry of baptizing the people with water. It was in the context of John's overall baptismal ministry for Israel that Jesus was baptized. Each of the four gospels presents Jesus' baptism in slightly different form, but all of them note the event as the starting point of Jesus' ministry, when the man who had worked and lived among his family, friends, and neighbors took on a new role. And my phrasing of that is part of the dilemma: Why do we believe that Jesus was not simply appointed for this role, chosen from of old, adopted as God's son, just as prophets, priests, and kings before him?

Luke describes the scene, saying that "when Jesus also had been baptized and was praying, the heaven was opened, and the Holy Spirit descended upon him in bodily form like a dove. And a voice came from heaven, 'You are my Son, the Beloved; with you I am well pleased.' " But what did it mean to say that Jesus was the Son of God? Is this a form of adoption or an identification of who Jesus not only is but always was? While the nation of Israel was the Lord's "first born son" (Exod 4:22) and, in Isaiah 1:2, 4, the people of Israel are referred to as God's children, individuals in Israel's past were also identified as sons of God, specifically the king, the son of David. For instance, in Psalm 2:7, God says to the king, "You are my son; today I have begotten you," while in Psalm 89: 27-29, the king is designated as the "firstborn" and promised that his line will be "established forever." In 2 Samuel 7:14, though, we find God speaking of the Messiah in parental terms: "I will be a father to him, and he shall be a son to me."

So when Jesus is also called "Son of God" in the baptism scene, reliant at least partially on Psalm 2:7 and other Old Testament passages and images, how do we know that when God calls him "my son," which will be repeated at the transfiguration, that this points beyond his human, Davidic status to a divine status? In some ways, I would argue, as the early Christians did at Nicaea, that it is not easily solved just on the basis of the passages themselves, which is precisely why we get back not just to language about Jesus but the experiences of those who followed him. After Jesus' death, his followers did not disband, did not skulk away shaken and disabused of their claims that this was the Messiah, but proclaimed that Jesus had been resurrected and was the Son of God, at the right hand of God, that is, divine in being.

This was Peter's claim when he first encountered Gentiles who experienced the gift of the Holy Spirit and were baptized into the church. Peter was stunned that the same Holy Spirit that descended on Jesus at his baptism and the Jewish disciples was now being poured out on Gentiles. Peter then began to comprehend: "I truly understand that God shows no partiality, but in every nation anyone who fears him and does what is right is acceptable to him." Why was God now available to all? Because the message of peace preached to Israel by Jesus Christ indicated that "he is Lord of all." God had indeed "anointed Jesus of Nazareth with the Holy Spirit and with power" at his baptism, as a sign that the incarnate son of God was now with them and this man was "Lord of all."

Reflect on God's words at Jesus' baptism. How does Jesus' sonship shape your understanding of God?

Turn Back to God

First Sunday of Lent

Readings: Deut 26:4-10; Ps 91:1-15;
Rom 10:8-13; Luke 4:1-13

*"Everyone who calls on the name of the
Lord will be saved."* (Rom 10:13)

Lent is a time to prepare for spiritual transformation, whether this will be signified by the sacraments of initiation at the Easter Vigil or by other rites and signs of conversion. But in order to prepare for transformation one must turn back to God. This is not easy, and those who have turned back to God sometimes feel at the same time the mysterious tug of evil, simultaneously so repellent and attractive.

In Exodus, the people of Israel, while enslaved in Egypt, turn to God in their suffering: "Out of the slavery their cry for help rose up to God. God heard their groaning, and God remembered his covenant with Abraham, Isaac, and Jacob. God looked upon the Israelites, and God took notice of them" (2:23-25). In chapter 26 of the book of Deuteronomy, Moses presents this same event to the people at the end of their long journey from slavery and wandering in the wilderness, recalling that "when the Egyptians maltreated and oppressed us, imposing hard labor upon us, we cried to the Lord, the God of our fathers, and he heard our cry and saw our affliction, our toil, and our oppression." The starting point for the liberation of the Israelites is the cry to God. There were, though, numerous temptations throughout these forty years, during which the Israelites, including Moses personally, stumbled. But Israel continued to get up and turn back to God.

Jesus, on the other hand, is presented in Luke as offering perfect resistance to wilderness temptation. Jesus "was led by the Spirit into the desert for forty days, to be tempted by the devil," a time period meant to recall the forty years the Israelites, led into the desert by God, stumbled and grumbled while wandering. The temptations the devil presents to Jesus in Luke's narrative mirror realities that tempt us all. The devil tempts Jesus during his fasting with material goods, in this case bread, the promise of earthly power and glory, and his own self-reliance by reciting words from the very source to which Jesus will turn to resist them—God's word.

Each time Jesus is tempted he turns to Scripture and finds his spiritual sustenance in passages precisely drawn from the texts that detail the time of the Israelites' wandering and stumbling. When tempted by bread, Jesus cites Deuteronomy 8:3, where Moses explains that reliance on manna taught the Israelites not to trust on bread alone but to be fed "by every word that comes from the mouth of the Lord." When offered power and glory if only he would worship the king of this world, Jesus turns to Deuteronomy 6:4-13 to stress the unique worship of God. The devil then cites Scripture back at Jesus (Ps 91:11-12), challenging and taunting him to put God to the test, to see if God is truly there for him. Jesus resists the temptation to use Scripture not as a sign of dependence upon God, but to satisfy his doubts. He cites Deuteronomy a third time—"do not put the Lord your God to the test" (6:16)—exhibiting his willingness to wait on God's plan and not to substitute his own schemes, a lesson drawn from the wandering of the Israelites in the desert.

Jesus' unique character and being allow him never to turn away from God, even in the face of stark temptation. He grounds his defiance of the devil, though, in the example of the lessons learned through the failings and persistence of the Israelites. They both become for us perfect models. The fact that the Scripture passages cited by Jesus all come from the time of the Israelites' wandering in the desert indicates that those lessons ought to remain a model for us, as they did for Jesus. In the face of temptation, one turns away from sin and turns back to God. One turns back to the events in which God raised up and sustained those who stumbled; one turns back to the Scriptures, which tell us to cry out to the Lord.

Spiritual transformation, though, is tricky business, and we may wish that our cry to the Lord would stick and that temptations and our willingness to indulge them would finally end. Yet our own stumbles, like those of the Israelites, make us no less worthy to call on God and turn back to him, again and again. God hears us and is waiting to prepare us for the Promised Land.

Imagine yourself in the desert with Jesus. What Scripture passages sustain you and have brought you to rely on God again and again?

CLOSE Encounters

Second Sunday of Lent

Readings: Gen 15:5-18; Ps 27:1-14;
Phil 3:17–4:1; Luke 9:28-36

"Master, it is good for us to be here." (Luke 9:33)

When God entered into a covenant with Abram, "a trance fell upon Abram, and a deep, terrifying darkness enveloped him." When Jesus took Peter, James, and John to the mountain to pray, "a cloud came and cast a shadow over them, and they became frightened when they entered the cloud." The terms of the covenant are not grounded in a gentleman's agreement or a polite handshake between equals. They embody a relationship between the people of God and the living God himself.

In this relationship God's whole being is present, including the reality of God's fearsome power. But if the encounters with God that sometimes mark the covenant are not "terms of endearment," neither should they be construed as ancient manifestations of "terrors of the covenant." These are the terms of the covenant.

Nothing new comes without change, and the necessary transformations bring fear and trepidation. The spiritual transformation essential for the people of God, however, requires the power and grace of God to be present in ways that overshadow human beings. Often these changes require suffering rooted in our own fear that we cannot change or cannot maintain faith in the ways of God.

Note, however, that although Abram and the apostles experienced the darkness, terror, and fear that accompanied the presence of God, this was not their entire experience of God. They did not flee. Peter, in fact, says, "Master, it is good for us to be here," and he is correct. Peter is sometimes mocked for speaking before thinking during the transfiguration. But when we consider what he says, he is correct that the good place, the best place, is in the presence of God.

Luke describes Peter as "not knowing what he was saying"; and this lack of "knowing" could describe either his need to say something in response to Jesus' glory or the inspiration to speak words whose full meaning was not apparent to him. Peter continues to speak, telling Jesus that three tents ought to be built for him, Moses, and Elijah. Some commentators have seen in this a desire to capture the experience and nail it down in place with secure tent pegs. But should we not want glory to dwell with us? Perhaps the problem with Peter's suggestion is that he can imagine only temporary dwellings, when God's glory is meant to dwell permanently among the people of God.

Peter also attempted too quickly to ground the glory of God in his midst by bypassing the spiritual transformation Jesus was to undergo before he could dwell in glory permanently. Moses and Elijah, the great representatives of the law and the prophets, appear to Jesus and speak to him about the "departure" he was about to "fulfill" in Jerusalem. In Greek, this departure is called *exodos.* Like the wandering Israelites, Jesus had much to suffer before he could enter the Promised Land. The word *exodos,* found only in Luke's account among the Synoptic Gospels, refers to the complex of events that would culminate in Jesus' ascension. There is no way to the ascension, however, without the crucifixion, the resurrection, and the preparation of the church for its own *exodos* into the world.

Exodus is spiritual transformation, but spiritual transformation is not easy, and only God's power and grace can truly transform us. Exodus also includes the fear of leaving behind what is good to forge onward for what is better. Peter was right; it was good that he and James and John were there to witness Jesus' glory, but there was more in store. That which would lead to permanent spiritual transformation for Jesus and his followers required an *exodos* that demanded suffering, fear, and terror. Peter desires three dwellings, with Jesus between Moses and Elijah, but the key verse in this regard might be Luke 23:33, in which Jesus hangs between two criminals, one on his left and one on his right.

"Master, it is good for us to be here," said Peter on the mountain, but the terms of the covenant required a transformation that would make suffering and sin themselves temporary dwellings on the exodus to glory.

Place yourself with Peter, James, and John on the mountain. Are you prepared to encounter God and to allow yourself to be transformed?

RePenT or PeRiSH

Third Sunday of Lent

Readings: Exod 3:1-15; Ps 103:1-11;
1 Cor 10:1-12; Luke 13:1-9

*"And all were baptized into Moses in the
cloud and in the sea."* (1 Cor 10:2)

Entering into the Catholic Church as an adult, as many are preparing to do during this Lenten season, is a movement of faith that takes time. Candidates often wonder if this is the "right" time or the "best" time, especially if painful misdoings within the church are being revealed to the public. As catechumens celebrate the scrutiny rites on this Third Sunday of Lent, they may even wonder whether they personally are worthy to make such a step.

But as the apostle Paul promises, "See, now is the acceptable time; see, now is the day of salvation!" (2 Cor 6:2). Catechumens often display the wonder of the initiate inexorably drawn to God, like Moses in Exodus 3, who wants to approach God yet still believes he is not worthy to carry out God's plan for him.

When God called Moses, one of the events on his résumé was murder. God's choice to appear to Moses and reveal his plans for Israel was not an imprimatur on previous behavior, but an acknowledgment that in a fallen world, all whom God calls have sinned. And yet with God's grace we are able to transcend our weaknesses and sins. God called Moses and revealed himself to Moses because God knew that Moses was able to carry out the mission God had planned for him. Moses was less certain.

When God appeared in the burning bush, Moses was drawn to the theophany; and when he came nearer, God announced his presence. God identified himself as "the God of Abraham, the God of Isaac, the God of Jacob," the God of his ancestors, but also as "I am who am"—a new name revealed to Moses. If the Israelites were to ask by whom Moses was sent, he was to tell them, "I AM sent me to you."

Moses did not agree immediately to represent God; he continued to question God's decision and whether he was the right person for the task. We all question God, both at points of initiation into the faith and at the revelation of new or deeper truths. Because the history of the covenant is a history of relationships, there is a record of questions people have asked of God: "Are you certain God? Is it me you want? Is this the path?"

Questions are essential to any relationship, but it is important that they not turn into obstinacy or willfulness when God's way has been revealed and the truth opened to us. God is merciful, gentle, and kind, but God ultimately must act if we do not. Questions can turn to grumbling against the ways of God; grumbling can turn to rejection of God. Paul speaks of grumbling against God's ways in the time of the Israelite wandering as a warning for the people of God.

When Jesus is told about some Galileans who had been killed by Pilate, he does not respond with the expected righteous indignation. Instead, as he often does, he turns the question to his interlocutors that asks them to look inward: "Do you think that because these Galileans suffered in this way they were worse sinners than all other Galileans? No, I tell you; but unless you repent, you will all perish as they did"!

It is a hard saying: Repent or perish. But both newly initiated and longtime disciples need the truth of the warning. God is gentle and merciful, and in his mercy will wait, since God desires that all should live in his presence.

As Jesus says in the parable of the Fig Tree, "Sir, leave it for this year also, and I shall cultivate the ground around it and fertilize it; it may bear fruit in the future." And if it does not? "If not, you can cut it down."

John the Baptist says at the beginning of Luke's gospel, to those who came to be initiated into the way of repentance: "Bear fruits worthy of repentance. Do not begin to say to yourselves, 'We have Abraham as our ancestor'; for I tell you, God is able from these stones to raise up children to Abraham" (Luke 3:8). It is true, of course, that God could raise up followers from stones, but God wants us. God hears our questions and waits on us but calls us to enter into his presence, to turn from sin and repent, to be near him.

As you think of God's call to repent, do you accept that God calls you as you are?

LOST and FOUND

Fourth Sunday of Lent

Readings: Josh 5:9-12; Ps 34:2-7;
2 Cor 5:17-21; Luke 15:1-32

"So if anyone is in Christ, there is a new creation." (2 Cor 5:17)

Is it necessary to be brought low, to fall to our knees, in order to grasp the love that God is always offering to us? No; it is not necessary that we hit rock bottom in worldly terms, but it is necessary to have grasped the spiritual reality that only with God is life the celebration of joy that was intended for us.

The parable of the Two Sons suggests that there is more than one way to wander away from God. In one of these ways the shock of God's absence comes like a revelatory bolt in the midst of suffering and loneliness. In the other the nearness of God is used to shield the distance and separation we have created from God's will for us. However we recognize the need to return to God, at the heart of our initiation into the church is the recognition that there is nothing we need more than the love of God, who gave his son, and "for our sake . . . made him to be sin who did not know sin, so that we might become the righteousness of God in him."

There is a false sophistication, manifested as ironic detachment or plain old cynicism, that sees human life as misery and unrelenting pain. But why is suffering more real than the love of God, which Jesus describes in the parable? Paul "implores us" to be "reconciled to Christ," to be a "new creation."

This simple description that Paul uses to describe the Christian life, "new creation," explodes from the page. The way of being in the world changes when new creation emerges, even if the world seems to be the same. Those in love understand Paul's formulation intimately: When in love, the world changes through the lover's transformation. When you are in love with Christ, there is a new creation.

It is not perspective alone that changes, however; it is the person who changes in light of God's love. It is true that one can wander from God's love, seek one's own path, see the world from the other side, and the entire time feel that one is still walking at God's side. This is the conundrum at the heart of Jesus' parable of the Two Sons. The one son, the younger, wanders far from the father, determined to assert his independence and do what he chooses with his inheritance. The other, the older son, stays close to his father, though infuriated by his own seeming subservience and, as it turns out, envious of his brother.

The one who wandered far off is brought low by his choices and finds himself humiliated by his circumstances. He vows to return home to serve as a servant in his father's home. But before he can even see his father, "while he was still a long way off, his father caught sight of him, and was filled with compassion."

The party was soon to begin when the older son, who had stayed home, heard about it. This son "became angry," and his father pleaded with him to no avail. The older son had already created a scenario in which his brother had "devoured your property with prostitutes," for he has not yet even greeted his returning younger brother, and now is being feted with a celebration.

For the person who is consciously drawing near to God for the first time, there can be a jolt of recognition on hearing this story. God has always been present, waiting for me. New creation is home. For the one who has turned from God, by taking God's presence and grace for granted, there must be an awakening, an acceptance that new creation is for all, both near and far: "My son, you are here with me always; everything I have is yours. But now we must celebrate and rejoice, because your brother was dead and has come to life again; he was lost and has been found."

The church calls out to those both near and far on behalf of a God whose compassion knows no bounds, as "ambassadors for Christ, as if God were appealing through us. We implore you on behalf of Christ, be reconciled to God." Come home, for the first time, or the thousandth time, because at the core of human existence is not cynicism but love, which stakes its claim on the Son who reached out for all of us from the cross.

Reflect on the parable of the Two Sons. Do you find yourself near to or far from God? What must you do to be at home with God?

THE LIFE OFFERED

Fifth Sunday of Lent

Readings: Isa 43:26-21; Ps 126:1-26;
Phil 3:8-14; John 8:1-11

"From now on, do not sin again." (John 8:11)

St. Augustine famously gave voice to his sins, who asked him, "Are you getting rid of us?" And "From this moment we shall never be with you again, not for ever and ever" (*Confessions* 8.10.26). The comfort of our sins is a mystery of human life. In order to turn away from them, to co-operate with God's grace, we must understand, intellectually but even more deeply spiritually, that the life God offers to us through Christ surpasses the momentary pleasures of a will turned away from God. The joy of a life lived in Christ not only transcends this temporal reality but gives depth to its genuine pleasures.

The Gospel of John presents us with a passage that is not found in the earliest manuscripts, but in which the church heard the authentic voice of Jesus. In it, a woman caught in adultery is brought forward to be stoned, and Jesus instructs the gathered crowd to "let anyone among you who is without sin be the first to throw a stone at her." The crowd went away, "and Jesus was left alone with the woman standing before him. Jesus straightened up and said to her, 'Woman, where are they? Has no one condemned you?' She said, 'No one, sir.' And Jesus said, 'Neither do I condemn you. Go your way, and from now on do not sin again.'" The passage is powerful, for Jesus asks us to place the weight of condemnation on ourselves, not on the other, and allows the woman, condemned under the law of Moses, to go. Even more powerful than punishment is Jesus' directive not to sin again.

This directive has at its core the fact that a life with God is more attractive than sin, that even if this woman, or you or I, were to stumble again, Jesus' message, "From now on do not sin again," remains not as a way to minimize sin, but as a way to maximize grace.

Paul knows the superior attraction of Christ, because as he says to the Philippians he regards "everything as loss because of the surpassing value of knowing Christ Jesus my Lord. For his sake I have suffered the loss of all things, and I regard them as rubbish, in order that I may gain Christ." The word translated as "rubbish," *skybala*, is actually a little earthier in Greek, too crude today to be found translated directly, but the comparison Paul makes is direct: what keeps me from knowing "Christ and the power of his resurrection" is meaningless in light of this goal toward which Paul presses on.

Paul moves on: "Forgetting what lies behind and straining forward to what lies ahead, I press on toward the goal for the prize of the heavenly call of God in Christ Jesus." As God says to the prophet Isaiah, "do not remember the former things, or consider the things of old. I am about to do a new thing; now it springs forth, do you not perceive it?"

In the scrutiny rite for catechumens on the Fifth Sunday of Lent, the goal for which Paul strains, the new thing that springs forth, the resurrection and the life, is foreshadowed in Jesus' raising Lazarus from the dead. Lazarus' illness, Jesus says, "does not lead to death; rather it is for God's glory, so that the Son of God may be glorified through it." In fact, Jesus delays his journey to see Martha, Mary, and Lazarus, "after having heard that Lazarus was ill," in order to make manifest God's glory through this "new thing."

Why then, when Jesus saw Mary and her friends crying, was he "greatly disturbed in spirit and deeply moved"? Why did Jesus weep? John tells us that Jesus was "greatly disturbed" when he came to the tomb, even though it was Jesus' plan to raise Lazarus.

Jesus here meets the reality of the pain and suffering created by sin, visible in the tears of those who, like Jesus, loved Lazarus. Here he stands before those who make manifest the very reason for which he became human.

The attractions of sin lead us to a fallen world that inexorably leads us to the grave. "From now on, do not sin again" is about turning from what draws us away from God and turning to "the resurrection and the life." Jesus says, "Those who believe in me, even though they die, will live, and everyone who lives and believes in me will never die. Do you believe this?"

Imagine yourself listening to Paul's letter read aloud in Philippi. Ask yourself: Do I seek Christ above all things? Do I consider Christ the greatest of all joys?

Palm Reading

Palm Sunday of the Lord's Passion

Readings: Isa 50:4-7; Ps 22:8-24; Phil 2:6-11;
Luke 19:28-40; Luke 22:14–23:56

"Blessed is the king who comes in the name of the Lord." (Luke 19:38)

The palm branches of Palm Sunday are mentioned specifically in John 12:13, and both Mark and Matthew describe people placing branches and cloaks on the ground as Jesus rode into Jerusalem, celebrating his entry with rejoicing and hailing him as king. Luke, on the other hand, describes the same procession but says only that cloaks were placed before Jesus. There is no need to doubt the presence of palm branches as Jesus rode into Jerusalem, but it is worthwhile to consider the purpose and symbolism of the branches in order to understand why Luke omits them from his account.

In the Old Testament, palm branches symbolize joy. In Leviticus 23:40 and Nehemiah 8:13-18, palm branches are associated with Succoth, the weeklong harvest festival of booths celebrated as a joyous pilgrimage while the temple was still standing. The palm branch could also be a symbol of victory. When the Maccabees took control of the citadel at the Jerusalem temple, "they entered it with praise and palm branches" (1 Macc 13:51). The palm branch was used in similar ways by Babylonians, Egyptians, Greeks, and Romans; and it was often a part of triumphant processions.

The themes of celebration and triumph are present when Jesus acts out the prophecy of Zechariah 9:9, in which the king rides into Jerusalem, humble and victorious, on a colt.

In the context of Jesus' entry into Jerusalem, Luke stresses that Jesus knew and was in control of his destiny. Jesus also knew that his entrance into the city, greeted deliriously by the crowds, was not the straightforward triumph for which others were hoping. Still, the crowds celebrated Jesus, with people "spreading their cloaks on the road," praising "God aloud with joy" and proclaiming, "Blessed is the king who comes in the name of the Lord." All these are actions that evoke not just Zechariah 9:9, but the processions of Solomon and Jehu in 1 Kings 1:32-40 and 2 Kings 9:1-13. The crowds welcome the Messiah into Jerusalem with unabashed joy.

Luke, however, is the only gospel in which not only are the palm branches missing, but in which opposition is shouted to Jesus as he enters the city. Luke has certain Pharisees call out to Jesus: "Teacher, rebuke your disciples." These Pharisees reject the acclamations praising Jesus and welcoming him as the messianic king. They feel bold enough to say this to Jesus as he rides into the city, perhaps thinking he will calm his followers down. Jesus responds, "I tell you, if they keep silent, the stones will cry out!" Jesus' words recall those of John the Baptist, who told the crowds coming to him for baptism not to presume upon the honor of birth, but to "bear fruits worthy of repentance," for "God is able from these stones to raise up children to Abraham." "These stones" represent not just the power of God over creation but the fact that even if some people will not grasp the reality of Jesus' kingship and celebrate it now, all creation will someday acknowledge Jesus as Lord. This recognition, Paul says, will be universal, "so that at the name of Jesus every knee should bend, in heaven and on earth and under the earth."

Those who waved the palm branches as Jesus entered Jerusalem welcomed in a king, though most could not have known the manner in which he would ascend to his throne. But why does Luke not mention the branches of victory and triumph? Perhaps Luke omits mention of the palm branches because the association of them with common expectations of victory and festivity seems out of place in the context of how Jesus will fulfill these hopes. Though all the gospel authors have Jesus ride into the city in fulfillment of Zechariah 9:9, Luke might associate the palm branches with the final, eschatological celebration of Christ's victory. Zechariah 14 envisions all the nations at the end of time in Jerusalem worshiping the king and celebrating Succoth, which includes the waving of palm branches. This image places Palm Sunday in religious and eschatological perspective: the entry into Jerusalem is a sign of Jesus' true kingship for those who will see, but not its final fulfillment.

Place yourself alongside Jesus as he rides into Jerusalem. How are my ideas about victory and triumph shaped by Jesus' life?

Encountering Hope

Easter Sunday

Readings: Acts 10:34-43; Ps 118:1-23;
Col 3:1-4; Luke 24:13-35

"The Lord has risen indeed, and he has appeared to Simon!"
(Luke 24:34)

"But we had hoped he was the one to redeem Israel." There it is, in a short summary sentence: the end of their hope. When hope is placed in the past tense, it is over. You get up, share a last word and embrace with your friends, dust yourself off and begin to walk home. The Greek tense of the verb "hope" in this sentence indicates ongoing action in the past ("we had been hoping"). The hope the disciples had placed in Jesus was not momentary, but was at the heart of their ongoing lives. Now, for Cleopas and the unnamed disciple, hope had crashed to a halt when Jesus died on the cross.

Jesus had told his apostles and disciples on a number of occasions that he would die and be raised, but either this did not meet their expectations or they were unable to process the truth Jesus had told them. The women, Mary Magdalene, Joanna, and Mary the mother of James, who had remained faithful to Jesus, were reminded of this truth when they went to care for Jesus' body at the tomb.

Two angels greeted them, saying: "Why do you seek the living one among the dead? He is not here, but he has been raised. Remember what he said to you while he was still in Galilee, that the Son of Man must be handed over to sinners and be crucified, and rise on the third day." Only then, Luke tells us, did the women remember what Jesus had said and believe what had taken place. But when the women went to tell the apostles and the other disciples what had happened, they were unable or unwilling to believe the women and considered their story "nonsense."

Permission must be granted for the doubt and reservations of the disciples, because, after all, dead men do not rise from their graves. When the teacher you had hoped was the Messiah dies a cruel Roman death on the cross, a death witnessed by many of his followers, you start to talk and discuss what might have been, how it went wrong, perhaps even how you could have been so mistaken.

The encounter of Cleopas and the unnamed disciple with the risen Lord on the road to Emmaus gives us insight into the nature of God and the means by which God came to save us and why it was so easy for the disciples to think in terms of hope in the past tense instead of joy in the present.

Apart from the humiliating death on the cross, there was no monumental rising from the grave, with strikes of thunder, lightning, earthquakes, and the resurrected Jesus striding triumphantly across the world stage. There was only an empty tomb and angelic messengers, witnessed by a few women and later by Peter, and quiet encounters along a lonely road.

Yet joy breaks in with the presence of the risen Lord quietly walking alongside his bereft disciples, asking questions and listening to their answers, until he breaks in and says, "Was it not necessary that the Messiah should suffer these things and then enter into his glory?" They do not directly identify the stranger as Jesus, but they want the stranger to remain near to them when he seems to be departing. They cannot be apart from this wondrous stranger. It is only when Jesus breaks bread with them that "their eyes were opened"—and he was gone.

Jesus was gone, but hope had returned. It is with hope that Cleopas and his friend returned to Jerusalem to meet with the other disciples. There they learned that their encounter with the risen Jesus was not the only one, as they are told that "the Lord has risen indeed, and has appeared to Simon!"

There could be no church without Easter, only broken disciples walking home with sweet and bitter memories; and there could be no Easter without Jesus risen from the dead. He can appear subtly and in numerous ways, but always in the breaking of the eucharistic bread that his disciples share. The mark of his disciples is hope and joy and the ability to say, "The Lord has risen indeed," for Jesus is present with them, and with us, along the way.

Walk alongside Cleopas, Jesus, and the unnamed disciple. When do you have trouble seeing the risen Lord?

A SHOCKInG LoVe

Second Sunday of Easter

Readings: Acts 5:12-16; Ps 118:2-24;
Rev 1:9-19; John 20:19-31

"Blessed are those who have not seen and yet have come to believe."
(John 20:29)

One of the most difficult things for Western Christians to grasp is the reality of the miraculous, which infuses the whole of the New Testament. We labor, more than we know, under the assumptions of a world that is a closed, empirical system from which God is absent. Rudolf Bultmann, the great twentieth-century biblical scholar, stated it clearly: "We cannot use electric lights and radios and, in the event of illness, avail ourselves of modern medical and clinical means and at the same time believe in the spirit and wonder world of the New Testament" (*New Testament and Mythology and Other Basic Writings* [Minneapolis: Fortress Press, 1984], 4).

Claims like this are believed widely today, even by Catholics, but it raises serious issues—primarily, what ought we to do with all the miracles in the New Testament? And if the miraculous is excised from the New Testament, what do we affirm as Christians?

Ben F. Meyer raised a different point in his book *The Aims of Jesus* (1979), asking whether "persons testifying to miracles are by that very fact shown to be incompetent or dishonest or self-deceived, and this without reference to their credentials or to the particulars of the case but by ineluctable a priori law" ([London: SCM Press, 1989], 101). This is an important point, for the first Christians who experienced and professed Jesus' resurrection, who were observers and performers of miracles, did not bear witness to these events as everyday occurrences but precisely as something out of the ordinary. These acts were understood as signs of God's divine act of salvation through Jesus Christ, not party tricks or magic acts. "If the salvific context is overlooked, the concrete possibility of miracle evaporates," wrote Meyer (101). But when we keep in mind the salvific context in which

God acted through the life, death, and resurrection of Jesus Christ, we have the context in which normal boundaries of human life were shattered on behalf of all humanity. The divine world is opened to us and the miraculous makes a claim on us.

Bultmann's claim is false, not just because today many people have made their peace with lightbulbs and miracles, robotic surgery and Peter's shadow healing the sick, but because it is false even in the ancient context.

The apostle Thomas's technology, oil lamps and papyrus, was superior to that which came before, but less advanced than what Bultmann knew and what we have today. It was not Thomas's technology, which was superior to that of the Bronze Age, that kept him from believing Jesus had been raised from the dead; it was his unwillingness to believe that God would act in such a way to bring about salvation. Technology is a red herring for a world closed off from the divine presence. Even in the first century, Thomas wanted empirical proof: "Unless I see the mark of the nails in his hands and put my finger into the nail marks and put my hand into his side, I will not believe."

Jesus appeared to him and to the others, passing through locked doors and otherwise breaking down the barriers between spirit and matter, saying to Thomas, "Put your finger here and see my hands, and bring your hand and put it into my side, and do not be unbelieving, but believe."

Thomas did not touch the risen Lord; but upon seeing him a lightbulb, or oil lamp, went off in his head and he said, "My Lord and my God!" Jesus had not broken through the technology of his day, but through the boundaries Thomas had placed on God's saving actions.

The very point of the incarnation is that something new has broken in on humanity, that a world we are tempted to see as closed, with God absent or indifferent, has been shocked open by God's love for us. Miracles are not intended to titillate or amuse us; they are signs to demonstrate God's care for us. Those who witnessed them passed them on so that we might believe, even though, or especially because, we have not seen the empirical proofs.

As you imagine Jesus' miracles, are there challenges in trying to understand and believe in the reality of God acting in history?

FISH FOR BREAKFAST

Third Sunday of Easter

Readings: Acts 5:27-41; Ps 30:2-13;
Rev 5:11-14; John 21:1-19

"Lord, you know everything; you know that I love you." (John 21:17)

It took the apostles some time to come to terms with the reality of Jesus raised from the dead; but once they accepted it, they had to face the challenges of day-to-day life in the context of their newly aroused faith. It was this tension between the mundane reality of ordinary life and the glorious reality of a Lord who now reigns with God that had to be resolved in the lives of the apostles. This tension was especially manifested in the apostles' personal encounters with the risen Lord, who challenged them to transform themselves in imitation of him.

The Gospel of John presents a scene at the Sea of Tiberias, where a number of Jesus' disciples had gathered. Jesus had already appeared to them twice, but Peter's mind that day was on fishing. Whether that is on his mind because he needs to earn some money, to relax and pray for a while, or just to catch some food to eat, Peter's announcement is matter of fact: "I am going fishing." Just as matter of fact is the response of the disciples, who say, "We will go with you."

One can imagine the disciples on the boat and what they might be discussing together; or perhaps they are silent, trying to process the events of Easter and what their next tasks might be. The revelation of Easter puts them between two worlds. Their discipleship with Jesus has not come to an end, but how will they begin again?

They fish all night without a catch and Jesus appears to them a third time at dawn. While they do not recognize him initially, they cast their net to the right side of the boat when he instructs them to do so. Only when they struggle to pull in their miraculous catch of fish do they recognize Jesus. What Jesus does next is ordinary; he feeds them breakfast, cooking some of the fish over a charcoal fire and giving them bread. He cares for them in the most ordinary of ways, helping with their work and giving them food to eat.

But after breakfast Jesus gives to Peter an extraordinary task: just as Jesus has fed his disciples, so Peter is now to feed his sheep. Jesus challenges Peter three times whether he loves him, and three times Peter answers yes, though he is "distressed that Jesus had said to him a third time, 'Do you love me?' and he said to him, 'Lord, you know everything; you know that I love you.' Jesus said to him, 'Feed my sheep.'" Jesus has challenged Peter three times to profess his love in light of Peter's threefold denial, but also to impress upon Peter his new vocation.

As simply as Peter said, "I am going fishing," Jesus now instructs him, "Feed my sheep." The Greek in this conversation is interesting, as Jesus asks Peter twice whether he loves him, using the verb *agapaô*, love that pours itself out for others, and Peter responds with *phileô*, the word for deep love between friends. On the third occasion, however, it is not Peter who alters the verb, but Jesus. Jesus aligns himself with Peter, using *phileô*, not *agapaô*, and Peter again responds with *phileô*, asserting that he loves Jesus deeply as a friend.

It is a subtle recognition by Jesus that the spiritual transformations necessary to follow him lie latent in our own gifts and abilities. Peter was called by Jesus to serve in a new way in order to feed his sheep, and his responses to Jesus indicated that he did not yet understand the full implication of this call even as he accepted it. Yet Jesus knew that these gifts lay dormant in Peter and he would be able to feed his sheep and follow him to death.

These latent gifts are made abundantly manifest in Peter's behavior in Jerusalem soon after the ascension. When Peter was told to stop preaching in Jesus' name, he responded, "We must obey God rather than any human authority." Not only will Peter pour himself out for the name of Jesus, but he will do so filled with joy. Just as Jesus knew, Peter's love for Jesus had grown so that now it fed not just his own needs but the needs of all of the disciples.

Sit with Jesus and the apostles as they eat breakfast together. How are you letting the extraordinary presence of Jesus suffuse your ordinary daily life?

THe GreaT MULTITUDE

Fourth Sunday of Easter

Readings: Acts 13:14-52; Ps 100:1-5;
Rev 7:9-17; John 10:27-30

"God will wipe away every tear from their eyes." (Rev 7:17)

It is easy to forget how few Christians there were when the church began. Acts 1:15 says there were 120 people gathered together after Pentecost. Acts also narrates the mass conversions of many people, sometimes in the thousands, but Robert M. Grant said that "one must always remember that figures in antiquity . . . were part of rhetorical exercises" (*Augustus to Constantine: The Rise and Triumph of Christianity in the Roman World* [Louisville, KY: Westminster John Knox Press, 2004], 7–8). These numbers are intended to indicate that the Holy Spirit was at work among the people, both in Jerusalem and increasingly in the Gentile world; they are not literal demographic data. Rodney Stark, a sociologist with expertise in religious conversion, has calculated that in the year 40 there might have been only one thousand Christians and by the year 100 only 7,530 (*The Rise of Christianity: A Sociologist Reconsiders History* [Princeton: Princeton University Press, 1996], 5).

While none of these numbers is exact, this inauspicious beginning renders the task of the church in these first decades even more remarkable. The church, formed after Easter in the certainty that Jesus Christ had been raised from the dead, was emboldened with a missionary impulse to be "a light to the Gentiles, that you may be an instrument of salvation to the ends of the earth." There are two things to keep in mind here. One was their wondrous realization that the message of salvation was for all peoples; the other was the shocking fact that it was the apostles and disciples of Jesus who would bring the gospel message to the whole world. Sometimes the early church faced opposition and persecution in preaching Jesus Christ, while at other times they faced indifference and ignorance.

Still, there were times when their message met willing hearers. Jesus said: "My sheep hear my voice; I know them, and they follow me. I give them eternal life, and they shall never perish." It was this message of eternal life that drew people to the church, but it was also the manner in which the early Christians lived out their lives. No matter the situations they faced, the early disciples of Jesus reflected a joy and faith that caused people to listen to them and to heed the call of the Christ. All who answered the call and belonged to the church, whether Jew or Gentile, no matter their station in life, were called to belong to one flock.

How does today's reading from the book of Revelation fit in the context of a practical survey of early Christian growth? While a difficult text to interpret, in one sense Revelation is always crystal clear: The hope of the church rests with the Lamb who was slain. This countercultural and counterintuitive victory was won by the sacrifice of the Lamb when it seemed the enemies of sin and death had triumphed. In John's visions, though, the Lamb is now seen enthroned and worshiped.

What is even more remarkable is that these visions reveal "a great multitude, which no one could count, from every nation, race, people, and tongue." But in the first century, no great multitude of people had yet been converted; there were not yet saints "from every nation, race, people, and tongue." John's vision represents not only the hope of eternal life but a sign of hope for the early church in their missionary task, which is a sign of hope for the whole world.

Before John had seen any practical evidence of the numerical success of the church, and even in the midst of persecution—he writes during his own exile of those "who have survived the time of great distress"—he envisions a spiritual reality of the joy of life "before God's throne" for a great multitude. This multitude, sheltered by God, "will not hunger or thirst anymore, nor will the sun or any heat strike them. For the Lamb who is in the center of the throne will shepherd them and lead them to springs of life-giving water, and God will wipe away every tear from their eyes."

It is this hope, carried by the first disciples, that made John's prophetic vision a reality. Multitudes would respond to the shepherd's voice, knowing that with him there would be comfort, every tear wiped away, safe in the presence of God for eternity.

Think about the vision of John in Revelation 7. How are you participating in the missionary task of the church?

LOVE WITHOUT CEASING

Fifth Sunday of Easter

Readings: Acts 14:21-27; Ps 145:8-13;
Rev 21:1-5; John 13:31-35

"I give you a new commandment: love one another." (John 13:34)

In preparation for his crucifixion, resurrection, and ascension, Jesus instructed his apostles on what their continuing mission would be when he was gone: "I give you a new commandment, that you love one another. Just as I have loved you, you also should love one another." This translation of the simple Greek passage, however, fails to reproduce an interesting element. Each of the secondary clauses is introduced by the Greek conjunction *hina*, which is usually translated "so that" or "in order that." Furthermore, the Greek text is all one sentence.

The passage as a result could also be translated, "I give you a new commandment, in order that you love one another, just as I have loved you, so that you also love one another." The conjunction *hina* points to the unity of the mission task and the desired goal of Jesus' commandment: you are to love in order to attain to love. Jesus concludes his commandment saying, "In this way, all will know that you are my disciples, if you have love for each other." Love is not just the commandment, but the fruit of the commandment.

In the same way, love is the fruit of Easter. It is God's love poured out for us that enables us to love one another. It is love that flourishes, however, not because suffering and pain have been banished in our present lives but in spite of the very real suffering we experience to the present day. Paul says to the early Christians in Galatia, "It is necessary for us to undergo many hardships to enter the kingdom of God." Paul and the early Christians were able to follow a rocky path with hope and faith because of the love they experienced in their midst through Christ.

This same love is able to sustain us still today as a foretaste and sign of the kingdom of God. All of us have suffered pain and loss, and all of us bear the scars of hurt; but it does not diminish the reality of anyone's suffering to say that some in the past and some today have suffered more than others. There are so many today who have experienced abuse, slavery, rape, and degradation for whom all seems lost. We must, of course, identify with all those who have suffered and who continue to suffer all forms of heartbreak day in and day out. We must work to change the conditions that allow such suffering to take place. Yet for all that we do, suffering mars lives and stalks survivors through endless days and nights. How can they know the healing power of love? The only way to know love is to experience it.

Only love can heal the wounds of injustice, however they are acquired. Injustice and evil leave deep scars on the soul that justice alone cannot heal. Justice can create good order and punish wrongdoers, but it cannot restore the soul to love. The irrationality of sin and evil leave behind time-bombs of antagonisms and hatreds, and nothing can heal these absurdities but love. Hope encourages us that against present evidence, life is worthwhile; faith instructs us that the solution to sin and suffering is available to all; but only love "will wipe every tear from their eyes."

When hope and faith pass away, Paul says in 1 Corinthians 13, love alone remains, the only theological virtue that is eternal. Love is the core of God's very being, the heart of Christ's incarnation, the comfort of the Holy Spirit and the purpose and result of our Christian life as disciples of Jesus. This is why Revelation describes heaven as life in the presence of God's love: "Behold, God's dwelling is with the human race. He will dwell with them and they will be his people and God himself will always be with them as their God. He will wipe every tear from their eyes, and there shall be no more death or mourning, wailing or pain, for the old order has passed away." As we await God's establishment of the new order, which is love, it is the task of the Christian to prepare by combating the old order through love. Once again our mission is the same as our goal: "Just as I have loved you, you also should love one another."

Reflect on Jesus' new commandment for his disciples. How are you showing love to those around you and to the world?

GOD'S GIFT FOR ALL

Sixth Sunday of Easter

Readings: Acts 15:1-29; Ps 67:2-8;
Rev 21:10-23; John 14:23-29

*"May the peoples praise you, O God;
may all the peoples praise you!"* (Ps 67:5)

The psalmist prays to God, "May your way be known upon earth; among all nations, your salvation." But how will this come to pass? Throughout the Old Testament, there are clues that someday, in some way, God's covenant will be expanded to welcome not just the descendants of Abraham but all the people of the world. Indeed, beginning with Genesis 22:18 and 26:4, Abraham and Isaac heard the promise that all nations would be blessed through their offspring. The early Christians came to believe through their experience of the teaching and life of Jesus, including his crucifixion and resurrection, that these promises would be enacted through the church. It was not clear to them, however, how such a world mission should be enacted, proof that Jesus did not leave for them a detailed twelve-point, five-year plan. It was even less clear that bringing the message of Jesus Christ to the world would entail a break with their fellow Jews.

We tend no longer to wonder that even the Gentiles could be saved; but then, when Peter recounted that the Holy Spirit had come to Cornelius and his family, "the circumcised believers who had come with Peter were astounded that the gift of the Holy Spirit had been poured out even on the Gentiles" (Acts 10:45). Still, Peter's shocking action had to be explained to his fellow believers, all of whom were Jews, and their response was wonder mixed with puzzlement: "Then God has given even to the Gentiles the repentance that leads to life."

Something new had broken in on the life of the Christian community, and not everyone was on board. The church met to make a decision on how Gentiles should be welcomed into the church, with the basic issue being whether they would have to follow the law of Moses just as every Jew did. Some of Jesus' disciples stated it this way: "Unless you are circumcised according to the custom of Moses, you cannot be saved." What we tend to forget is that this position made sense according to all the clearest claims of Scripture and tradition.

Yet Peter, Paul, and others had seen the work of the Holy Spirit among the Gentiles and found Scripture spoke in a new way to a new situation. The church as a whole decided, in what today is called the Jerusalem Council, not to require Gentiles to follow all of the law of Moses, but to adhere only to certain restrictions regarding sexual practice, idolatry, and food. This decision seems logical to us today, even "the way it has always been," though in reality it reflected a decision that required startling change in practice and understanding. What the early church came to understand, though, was that if Christ was to be for all, Christ would need to be made available to all on the same terms. It was not simply a practical decision, but the reality of God working in and speaking to the church.

In the reading from the book of Revelation, John's vision of the New Jerusalem includes the Jewish imagery of the temple with the provocative newness of the Christian understanding. John reports, "I saw no temple in the city, for its temple is the Lord God the Almighty and the Lamb." The temple, grounded in the locality of Jerusalem, was now spiritualized to indicate the divine home of all people encompassing the whole cosmos.

The Gospel of John reflects elements of this vision when it says (in the NRSV translation) that "those who love me will keep my word, and my Father will love them, and we will come to them and make our home with them." The NAB translation better reflects the Greek: "We will come to him and make our dwelling with him." The new temple, the New Jerusalem, will be with each person, regardless of where they were from or where they once dwelled, because God will be all in all. The church, experiencing the salvation of God in its midst, began to live out a promise, now made new.

As you experience God dwelling with you even now, how do you sense God doing something new in your midst today?

Heaven-sent

The Ascension of the Lord

Readings: Acts 1:1-11; Ps 47:2-9; Eph 1:17-23 or
Heb 9:24-28; 10:19-23; Luke 24:46-53

*"Men of Galilee, why do you stand looking
up towards heaven?"* (Acts 1:11)

Paul says of Jesus in 1 Corinthians 15:45, "Thus it is written, 'the first man, Adam, became a living being'; the last Adam became a life-giving spirit.'" Luke Timothy Johnson draws on this verse when he describes the ascension of Jesus, saying that "the 'withdrawal' of Jesus is not so much an absence as it is a presence in a new and more powerful mode: when Jesus is not among them as another specific body, he is accessible to all as life-giving spirit" (*The Gospel of Luke*, Sacra Pagina series, ed. Daniel J. Harrington [Collegeville, MN: Liturgical Press, 1991], 406).

While it is true that Jesus is now with us "as life-giving spirit," even after his ascension, he remains a particular person, both God and man. While he is present in a new and more powerful mode, Jesus is absent in a profound way, which is why we yearn for his return. At the ascension Jesus does not cease to be the one who came to earth, who was raised up and who will come again in glory to judge both the living and the dead. This is the same risen Lord who appeared after his ascension to Paul. Paul asked in response to his experience, "Who are you Lord?" "I am Jesus, whom you are persecuting" (Acts 9:5).

At the same time, we must acknowledge the constant presence of Jesus in the church and his accessibility to all of us. It is through the Eucharist that we know Jesus intimately now and as a foretaste of heaven; it is in the church, the Body of Christ, of which he is the head, that he is truly present in our midst. The tension between Jesus' presence and absence exists also in our conception of the ascension. The ascension is described in Luke and Acts using the cosmological language of a three-tiered universe, in which Jesus floats up into heaven—an image long ago exploded by scientific views of the cosmos. But if we speak of the imagery of the ascension as a metaphor, this should not divert us from the reality of the event: Jesus exists in his bodily particularity with God.

In asserting Jesus' identity and real existence, we support the hopeful anthropology of Christianity against gnostic devaluations of personal identity and the goodness of the body. As the risen Jesus exists even now as Lord, we too will one day be raised up as physical beings with personal identity. We will not be subsumed in a divine nothingness; we will not lose our individuality. Yet a radical transformation will occur between who we are now and who we will be in heaven.

There might be some people who withdraw from the notion of heaven as a "place," but Christianity does not reduce the afterlife to psychological projection or childish wish-fulfillment. Christianity speaks of the existence of these places and those who inhabit them as real. Such notions are not simply metaphors, but they call on us to move from our concrete notions of spirit and matter to a more subtle if unclear notion of the nature of ultimate reality. The reality of the ascension is at the heart of the Christian life and the Christian hope. It is the point at which the church begins to take shape as eucharistic community—that is, centered on *koinonia*, fellowship or communion, and the Eucharist. It is a sign of the hopeful and joyful anthropology of the church, which promises not a melting away of our personhood, but the continuation of our identity as radically transformed beings in God's presence. And the ascension is the event that makes us aware of Jesus' presence and his absence. It is, finally, the promise of Jesus' return in his particularity as the risen Lord: the one who became incarnate on our behalf, who died on the cross for us, who was raised from the dead and sits at the right hand of the Father and who will return to be present with us.

Watch with the disciples as Jesus ascends. How do you experience the absence and the presence of Christ today?

Jesus is Lord

Seventh Sunday of Easter

Readings: Acts 7:55-60; Ps 97:1-9;
Rev 22:12-21; John 17:20-26

*"I see the heavens opened and the Son of Man standing
at the right hand of God!"* (Acts 7:56)

It remains baffling and astounding even today to think about the first disciples of Jesus and their understanding that Jesus is Lord. It was only in the context of the resurrection that devoted Jewish monotheists began to consider that the nature of the one God was other than they had formerly considered. But what does it mean to say that their reconsideration took place "in the context of the resurrection"? The basis for this reconsideration can be expressed simply in one word: experience. Jesus had lived and died with his disciples around him, his body breaking like any other from the nails, whips, and the rough wood of the cross. His human body bore the afflictions of violence like any other human body. Those who saw his body and laid it in the tomb knew that he was dead.

It was the experience of the risen Jesus, not as a phantom or a memory, but as the person Jesus that led to the belief in the resurrection. Experience drove conviction. But it was the continued experiences of the disciples that led them to reflect on who the Messiah truly was, not just their good teacher raised from an inglorious death, but somehow, in some way, the Lord. The deacon Stephen, "filled with the Holy Spirit . . . gazed into heaven and saw the glory of God and Jesus standing at the right hand of God. 'Look,' he said, 'I see the heavens opened and the Son of Man standing at the right hand of God!'" This was not Stephen's attempt to rile up his compatriots, but an expression of his spiritual experience. In the midst of his martyrdom, Acts reports that Stephen prayed, "Lord Jesus, receive my spirit," mimicking Jesus' own words to God on the cross in Luke 23:46—"Father, into your hands I commend my spirit"—and commending his own spirit to Jesus not the Father. By so doing, Stephen implicitly equated the Father and the Son as persons of the Godhead.

It was this very equation that aroused the violence against Stephen, in the same way that such claims arouse derision and even violence against Christians today in some regions, but what options are there when one has experienced the truth? Like all of the first Christians, Stephen revered the one true God, whom the psalmist hymns as "most high over all the earth" and "exalted far above all gods." Those who worship idols "are put to shame" for "all gods bow down before him." For those who had not experienced the risen Jesus as Lord, the claims of the early Christians must have seemed like idolatrous claims, attempts to place Jesus in a new pantheon.

Yet, one of the things that stands out about Christian claims about the divinity of Jesus is that Jesus is not seen as God in addition to the Father or instead of the Father, but *with* the Father. Jesus is Lord precisely because the one true God has revealed something about the nature of God and the nature of the Godhead in the risen Jesus. Just as Stephen saw Jesus "standing at the right hand of God," so John in his visions of the Apocalypse sees the Father and the Lamb, Jesus, on the throne together, so that Jesus is now understood to be "the Alpha and the Omega, the first and the last, the beginning and the end" not in competition with the Father but as a true revelation of the one God.

John's gospel explicates the reason for this revelation, and perhaps the reason for the manner of this revelation of Jesus as Lord, in one of the chapters known as the Farewell Discourses. Jesus was sent to reveal through his incarnation the nature of God's love for humanity. Jesus says that "as you, Father, are in me and I am in you, may they also be in us, so that the world may believe that you have sent me. The glory that you have given me I have given them, so that they may be one, as we are one, I in them and you in me, that they may become completely one, so that the world may know that you have sent me and have loved them even as you have loved me." In God deigning to come to humanity in the incarnation, God's love for humanity was made known as well as the triune nature of God and God's desire that as Jesus became human, so God desires that we ultimately become like God. As Jesus says, "may they also be in us."

How does the nature of God's revelation in Jesus instruct you about God's love of humanity?

Reborn in the Spirit

Pentecost Sunday

Readings: Acts 2:1-11; Ps 104:1-34;
1 Cor 12:3-13; John 20:19-23

"For in one Spirit we were all baptized into one body." (1 Cor 12:13)

The Jewish feast of Pentecost, also known as the Feast of Weeks, originally celebrated the spring harvest. It was a pilgrimage festival that took place fifty days after the end of Passover. By the time of Jesus Pentecost was also celebrated as a joyous remembrance of the giving of the law at Sinai. Seen together, the two aspects of the Jewish festival give thanks to God for feeding both body and spirit. The Christian commemoration of Pentecost would adopt and transform these two elements.

The first Christian celebration of Pentecost took place as the believers came to terms with the reality and resonance of Christ's absence and simultaneous presence among them, but also in the midst of their unity, since they were still "all together in one place." In the Gospel of John, Jesus promised his apostles that "the Advocate, the Holy Spirit, whom the Father will send in my name, will teach you everything, and remind you of all that I have said to you" (14:26). It was during their Pentecost gathering that the church, the Body of Christ, experienced the reality that Jesus had promised them prior to his ascension, when the Spirit came upon them in wind, fire, and voice.

The gift of the Holy Spirit that the church experienced was a sign that the promises of the prophets had come to fruition through the mission of the Messiah Jesus. As Jesus was now enthroned at the right hand of God, the coming of the Spirit indicated not just the fruits of salvation given to each Christian, but the church as the means by which this salvation would be made known in the world. At its core the communion of the Holy Spirit is ecclesial and essential for the church to fulfill its own earthly mission.

At Pentecost the body of believers began to restore the unity intended for humanity. In a sort of reversal of the story of the Tower of Babel, each believer spoke a spiritual language that Jews from all over the world heard in their own language. The Spirit spoke a language that allowed the church to envision a future in which all humanity is brought to a true worship of God. Like the law given at Sinai to feed the people of Israel, at this new Pentecost God gave the Holy Spirit to the church to feed the Body of Christ.

Though the Holy Spirit does not always come in manifestations of ecstasy, which the people of Jerusalem wrote off as drunkenness, the Holy Spirit is always present. The apostle Paul concentrates on the multifaceted and multi-gifted nature of the church. At the heart of the Spirit's gift is the foundational proclamation that "Jesus is Lord" because this witness binds us together as members of Christ's body, whoever we are and from wherever we come, for we have all been "baptized into one body—Jews or Greeks, slaves or free—and we were all made to drink of one Spirit."

Even more, by virtue of our drinking of the one Spirit, we are united in the Body of Christ through our diversity of gifts. It seems counterintuitive, but it is not. Unity is opposed to uniformity, diversity to division. The church must be united and diverse, which gives us all access to the deep well of the Spirit's variety of gifts. As Paul says, not all will speak in tongues; but each gift, which is in reality each unique person, is essential to the church. In a fallen world of bullying, ostracism, and fear, people can fall away from community and into loneliness, but the church must be a bulwark against these wounds to the body of humanity and the Body of Christ. Each of us has a spiritual gift to offer to the church, for Paul tells us that "to each is given the manifestation of the Spirit for the common good." It is our ecclesial task, as a people reborn in the Spirit, not just to feed the world with our own gifts but to open our eyes to the gifts of the Spirit, which God has given to and activates in every person, that we might be fed by our brothers and sisters for whom we have not yet found a place at the table.

Imagine yourself at the first Pentecost in Jerusalem or listening to Paul in Corinth. When have you experienced the joy of your spiritual gifts and the gifts of others?

GOD In ReLaTIOnSHIP

The Solemnity of the Most Holy Trinity

Readings: Prov 8:22-31; Ps 8:4-9;
Rom 5:1-5; John 16:12-15

"[I was] delighting in the human race." (Prov 8:31)

The mystery at the heart of human life is discovered in our relationships, whose outlines might be simply explained but which are ineffable at the core. How we love and live for one another defies description. We struggle for words to make real what we know through experience. When one of my sons as a small boy told me, "I want you to live longer than anyone else," he expressed his love as a desire that our lives together should continue on and on without end. This being for and with one another takes us to the mystery of Christian life.

God in Christianity is a supernatural mystery; and in the depth of God's mysterious being, we discover the reality of the Trinity. God exists in relationship as Trinity and God exists in relationship with humanity, telling us through our very creation that God wants our lives together to continue on and on without end.

In Scripture, the reality of God as Trinity is revealed through the language of relationship. In the book of Proverbs, Wisdom describes herself as God's "master worker . . . daily his delight, / rejoicing before him always, / rejoicing in his inhabited world." While Wisdom is not necessarily identified with a particular person of the Trinity, Proverbs expresses the reality of God in communication, who takes joy in creation. This delight points to the gratuitousness of creation, for the God who exists in perfect communion as triune lacks nothing, but brings humanity into being for God's and our good pleasure. These same mysteries appear more fully in the New Testament, not as doctrinal or creedal statements, but as the reality of God experienced in the lives of the first believers.

Paul's words to the Romans outline the nature of God by virtue of the relationship Paul has entered into with the living God. Paul explains that

Christians have gained "peace with God through our Lord Jesus Christ, through whom we have gained access by faith." Later Paul states that "we boast in hope of the glory of God . . . and hope does not disappoint, because the love of God has been poured out into our hearts through the Holy Spirit that has been given to us."

Within this short passage, Paul has mentioned the relationships among God the Father, Jesus Christ, and the Holy Spirit and how through them we are given peace, hope, and love. Though the word *trinity* is never mentioned, the Trinity reveals itself to Paul through the experience of God's being.

Jesus spoke of God's relational essence as he prepared the apostles for his departure. The Holy Spirit would guide the disciples "to all truth." But this truth that the Spirit speaks, Jesus says, is not the Spirit's "own" but is intended to enlighten believers and to glorify Jesus and the Father as well, for "everything that the Father has is mine." In perfect communion, the Trinity, three persons in one nature, reveals the mystery of perfect relationship: giving of oneself perfectly for the other, in order to bring all of us into the glory of God.

Even with this revelation of God's inner life and God's love poured out for us, it is impossible to truly describe in rational terms the nature of the Trinity. It is the revelation itself of the Trinity, and the experience of the Trinity, that makes it real for us; however we struggle to describe that God is three persons in one nature, that one person became human for us and that God desires that we share in the life of the Trinity.

Still, there is a parallel with human relationships and the way we come to know human beings. We can describe the visible form of persons, the behaviors that show who they are, but it is in being with them that we experience their essence, which concepts and words cannot capture. It is simply that in their presence one experiences love that in a moment becomes unending. God delights in these moments within the eternity of the triune mystery and for reasons that are inexplicable invites us to share in this life forever, telling each of us in fact that "I want you to live longer than anyone else."

Prayerfully reflect on your relationship with the triune God. How has your appreciation for the Trinity grown and deepened over the years?

THE FOOD OF LIFE

The Solemnity of the Most Holy Body
and Blood of Christ

Readings: Gen 14:18-20; Ps 110:1-4;
1 Cor 11:23-26; Luke 9:11-17

"And all ate and were filled." (Luke 9:17)

Body and blood, bread and wine—these are basic components of the human being and the stuff that sustains human life. These basic and foundational realities speak to the ordinary humanity of Jesus and one of the deepest mysteries of the church. Without the incarnation, we could not speak of Jesus' body and blood. Without Jesus' sacrifice on the cross, we could not be offered these simple elements transformed into the Body and Blood of Christ. In the Eucharist we participate in the whole of Jesus' life, as human and divine, as victim and priest, who offers us sustenance under the appearances of bread and wine.

In one miracle account in Luke, a story recounted in all four gospels, Jesus feeds the hungry after teaching "the crowds about the kingdom of God" and healing "those who needed to be cured." In these two ways Jesus met their spiritual needs; but as the day draws to a close, his apostles encourage Jesus to send the people away so that they can find places to sleep and eat and meet their physical needs. Jesus instead challenges his apostles to "give them some food yourselves." The verb Jesus uses is in the imperative, the messianic equivalent of "Just do it!" "You feed them!" When the apostles point to the impracticalities of Jesus' request—"five loaves and two fish are all we have," and there were five thousand men, not counting women and children—Jesus just does it, though he engages the help of his apostles.

Jesus has the apostles divide the crowd into groups of fifty and then, "taking the five loaves and the two fish, he looked up to heaven, and blessed and broke them, and gave them to the disciples to set before the crowd. And all ate and were filled." We should not overlook the physical nature of this miracle. People need bread for their bodies; but the eucharistic overtones are present throughout the blessing, breaking, and distribution of the bread. Indeed, when the apostles picked up the leftovers "they filled twelve wicker baskets." This is not an insignificant detail, but speaks to the church's task to feed the physical and spiritual needs of people and to know that through Christ there is an abundance of food available.

But this miracle does point toward Jesus' continuing to feed us, through the church, in the Eucharist. Paul recites the words from the Last Supper in which Jesus gave his body and blood for our salvation, which we consume under the appearances of bread and wine. Paul also recites the words of Jesus that this participation in the Eucharist is a remembrance, or anamnesis, that is, a commemoration, memorial, and representation of Christ's sacrifice. The anamnesis has two elements. Most prominent is Jesus' sacrifice on behalf of humanity; less prominent, but not to be overlooked, is Jesus' feeding of the multitudes in order to fulfill their human needs.

Yet this is not all. Paul states that "as often as you eat this bread and drink the cup, you proclaim the death of the Lord until he comes." As Jesus fed the earthly multitude, as he feeds us now in the Eucharist, so he will join us in the eschatological banquet, when "many will come from east and west" and "eat with Abraham and Isaac and Jacob in the kingdom of heaven" (Matt 8:11). The Eucharist is therefore a proclamation of the coming kingdom of God, when we will eat in the messianic banquet the heavenly food of which what we now consume is a foretaste. At that time, every aspect of the eucharistic feast—as memorial, real presence, and eschatological proclamation—will be fulfilled. In the meantime, as we remember, proclaim, and await, we recall, too, Jesus' words at the miraculous feeding of the crowds: "You feed them!" This imperative is bequeathed to the church through the actions of the priest in the Eucharist and through each one of us as we attempt to meet the physical and spiritual needs of those who hunger in every way, for the bread of today and for the bread of tomorrow. We call all to the table, for Christ will feed all who come, and there will always be enough.

Imagine yourself being fed by Jesus, either with the multitude of five thousand or today. What do you want to say to him for the food you have been given?

Queen of Heaven

The Assumption of the Blessed Virgin Mary

Readings: Rev 11:19a; 12:1-6a, 10ab; Ps 45:10, 11, 12, 16;
1 Cor 15:20-27; Luke 1:39-56

"A great portent appeared in heaven:
a woman clothed with the sun." (Rev 12:1)

On November 1, 1950, Pope Pius XII wrote that "by the authority of our Lord Jesus Christ, of the Blessed Apostles Peter and Paul, and by our own authority, we pronounce, declare, and define it to be a divinely revealed dogma: that the Immaculate Mother of God, the ever Virgin Mary, having completed the course of her earthly life, was assumed body and soul into heavenly glory" (*Munificentissimus Deus*, 44). Why was this dogma pronounced and declared? When Reinhold Niebuhr was asked by Paul Tillich a few months before the promulgation of the decree if he thought the pope would declare the assumption of the Blessed Virgin Mary a dogma, the Protestant theologian was reported to have said, "I don't think so; he is too clever for that; it would be a slap in the face of the whole modern world and it would be dangerous for the Roman Church to do that today" (Paul Tillich, *A History of Christian Thought: From its Judaic and Hellenistic Origins to Existentialism* [New York: Scribner, 1972], 224).

The declaration of the assumption of the Blessed Virgin Mary makes no sense in terms of the whole modern world, or any other age, until you place it in the context of eternity, our destiny in heaven, and realize how little sense it makes to imagine any of us pure and holy and dwelling forever in God's presence. It is a sign not just of Mary's obedience to God's will as the Theotokos, but a divine gift to Mary of the most bountiful God, the most generous God, which is in fact the English translation of the title of Pope XII's encyclical *Munificentissimus Deus*. And the divine gift of God to Mary is not only a sign of Mary's unique role in salvation history and her holiness but a sign for all of us who yearn for eternity in the presence of God.

For instance, *Munificentissimus Deus* speaks of the "privileges and prerogatives" granted to Mary by God's "sovereign generosity" (3), that by "an entirely unique privilege" she "completely overcame sin by her Immaculate Conception" (5), and that "God, the King of the universe" granted Mary "favors that surpass nature. As he kept you a virgin in childbirth, thus he has kept your body incorrupt in the tomb and has glorified it by his divine act of transferring it from the tomb" (18). While Mary received these privileges, prerogatives, and favors due to her divine motherhood, her holiness, her relationship with her son Jesus, and her Son's love for his mother, they could only be granted to her by God who brings Mary, as we all hope we might be too, to her heavenly home.

Mary, as all of us, relies upon God for her salvation, even when she acts in unison with that divine will. Mary had "that most perfect grace" because it was granted to her by God and it was a "special blessing" of God "that countered the curse of Eve" (*Munificentissimus Deus*, 27). The culmination of that privilege was that Mary was taken, free from corruption, to the perfection of heaven where she is designated by the church Queen of Heaven, deriving this designation from the image of the woman clothed with the sun "and on her head a crown of twelve stars," in Revelation 12:1.

But Mary's life in heaven now is the life for which all disciples of Jesus hope. Indeed the encyclical of Pope Pius XII intended to increase hope in all the members of the church so "that those who meditate upon the glorious example Mary offers us may be more and more convinced of the value of a human life entirely devoted to carrying out the heavenly Father's will and to bringing good to others" (*Munificentissimus Deus*, 42). The encyclical desires to combat the "illusory teachings of materialism," in particular, by drawing out through the teaching of the assumption of Mary that all of our souls and bodies are destined for eternity and that our own belief in the resurrection would be strengthened.

As Mary herself says in the *Magnificat*, "He has helped his servant Israel, / in remembrance of his mercy, / according to the promise he made to our ancestors, / to Abraham and to his descendants forever" (Luke 1:54-55). We are those descendants, intended to share in the promises to Abraham. Over sixty years after the assumption of Mary was promulgated as dogma, this whole modern age needs to be reminded again and again that not just Mary, Queen of Heaven, but all of us are intended for eternity, body and soul, transformed into the likeness of God, as Mary already has been by the mercy and generosity of God.

As you ponder the mystery of Mary's assumption into heaven, how does this teaching increase your hope in the resurrection? Are you able to accept that you, not just soul but body too, are intended for eternity with God in heaven? How does Mary's life in heaven help you to imagine your intended future with God and the saints?

WHAT WE WILL BE

The Solemnity of All Saints

Readings: Rev 7:2-14; Ps 24:1-6;
1 John 3:1-3; Matt 5:1-12

"What we will be has not yet been revealed." (1 John 3:2)

At the end of Paul's first letter to the Thessalonians, in 5:23-24, he prays for the church that "the God of peace" may "himself sanctify you entirely; and may your spirit and soul and body be kept sound and blameless at the coming of our Lord Jesus Christ. The one who calls you is faithful, and he will do this." This passage places a new emphasis on the tension between the indicative (what we are) and the imperative (what we are to be) in the Christian life. However mightily we struggle for holiness in this world, as is our Christian call and duty, it is God who will "himself sanctify you entirely." It is God who calls us to live in eternity alongside the saints and "the one who calls you is faithful, and he will do this."

That God will do this is seen in the image from Revelation of "a great multitude that no one could count, from every nation, from all tribes and peoples and languages, standing before the throne and before the Lamb, robed in white, with palm branches in their hands." Holiness is intended not for the few, but for a great multitude. This is truly good news, for, as it says in the KJV version of Romans 8:31, "If God be for us, who can be against us?" Ultimately, in the journey to holiness, it is our own will turned against God that is the stumbling block on our path to eternity, not God who desires us to be formed more and more into God's own likeness.

This is why the growth of holiness is a task in which we share the work with God as we prepare for our eternal life. It is not the work of "earning" heaven, but of turning to God to prepare ourselves to live in the glory of eternity, something that can never be earned, but is gracefully given to us by God who will himself sanctify us entirely. As we work to become more like God in this life, we are given clear directives for behavior generally and specifically.

The psalmist asks, "Who shall ascend the hill of the Lord? And who shall stand in his holy place?" An answer is offered, "Those who have clean hands and pure hearts, who do not lift up their souls to what is false, and do not swear deceitfully. They will receive blessing from the Lord, and vindication from the God of their salvation. Such is the company of those who seek him, who seek the face of the God of Jacob." Some behaviors are specifically noted to avoid, such as falsehood and deceitful swearing, but the general stance of those who seek holiness is to "seek the face of the God of Jacob," to always make the pursuit of God, who is holy, their life's pursuit above all else.

In the Beatitudes in Matthew, Jesus offers that we seek the face of God when we, among other things, "hunger and thirst for righteousness," when we are pure in heart, when we are merciful, when we are peacemakers, and when we are "persecuted for righteousness' sake." The ultimate result of turning to God in our daily life is that the disciples of Jesus "will see God," "will be called children of God," and will receive the kingdom of heaven. This is what it means to be a saint: to seek God in each of our daily actions, to so grow in holiness that we want each choice we make, each word we speak to draw us and others to the face of God and so become more fully each day children of God.

It is God's love that draws us to God, and that allows us to act in love for those who are unlovable, poor, and weak, who the powerful and wealthy no longer see as worthwhile. Love allows us to see the true worth of every human as a creation of God, made in the image of God, intended to live in God's presence for eternity. As John writes, "see what love the Father has given us, that we should be called children of God; and that is what we are." Already we are God's children, formed in love to act with love. Our destiny remains opaque, unclear, but every act of holiness turns us to God. Finally, though, God will do it and reveal it to us: "What we do know is this: when he is revealed, we will be like him, for we will see him as he is. And all who have this hope in him purify themselves, just as he is pure." We live like saints, in order that God will sanctify us entirely. And God will do it. It is the purpose for which we were created.

While we do not know exactly what life in God's presence will be like, each act of holiness turns us to become more and more like God. In what ways have you been able to live out the life of holiness most fully? Are there ways in which you struggle to live out the call to holiness? When you think of your life with God and the saints, what do you imagine it will be like?

WEDDING PARTY

Second Sunday in Ordinary Time

Readings: Isa 62:1-5; Ps 96:1-10;
1 Cor 12:4-11; John 2:1-11

"As the bridegroom rejoices over the bride,
so shall your God rejoice over you." (Isa 62:5)

Spousal or nuptial imagery runs throughout the whole of the Bible, sometimes reflecting the painfulness of marriage between God and the beloved Israel, though more often speaking of the shared joy of the beloved couple and the still greater joy to come. Isaiah first mentions those times when Israel was called "forsaken" and the land "desolate." It hearkens to the language of the prophet Hosea when he says "plead with your mother, plead— for she is not my wife, and I am not her husband— that she put away her whoring from her face, and her adultery from between her breasts" (Hos 2:2). The crushing experience of love betrayed and lost is on full display here. It resonates with readers ancient and modern because even if we have not experienced the same despair of the heartbroken lover, though many of us have, we know someone who has felt the sting of loss or in the lows of our relationships worried that it might be us.

Hosea goes on to promise Israel, though, that "I will take you for my wife forever; I will take you for my wife in righteousness and in justice, in steadfast love, and in mercy. I will take you for my wife in faithfulness; and you shall know the Lord." Isaiah echoes this promise, saying to Israel, "you shall be called My Delight Is in Her, and your land Married; for the Lord delights in you, and your land shall be married. For as a young man marries a young woman, so shall your builder marry you, and as the bridegroom rejoices over the bride, so shall your God rejoice over you." The remarkable image here is of a relationship made fresh, the past forgotten, as the bridegroom, again now a young man, looks upon his bride, made new as a young woman, with the eyes of new love. Let your favorite wedding photo flash before your eyes here, as you reflect on the hope and promise of new love in the faces of the young, newly married couple.

Let that image remain as you picture an ancient wedding in Cana. The wedding feast in antiquity was a time of community and family celebration. Though ancient nuptials are often presented as marriages of convenience, binding family and fortune together, there is no question that they were times of great joy, anticipation, and even romantic love. Remember Isaiah's word that "as the bridegroom rejoices over the bride, so shall your God rejoice over you." The only reason this rejoicing strikes home for readers in the past is because they know the joy of the young married couple.

Mary, Jesus, and his disciples were invited to a wedding. Unfortunately for the family and the guests the wine ran out. Would the celebration come to a quick end? Mary alerts her son to the fact and ultimately he, with her encouragement and intervention, acts to bring this sad situation to an end. The actual miraculous action that the Gospel of John reports says that "there were six stone water jars for the Jewish rites of purification, each holding twenty or thirty gallons," which will be plenty of wine, an abundance of wine, even for a large community wedding. We might be tempted to rename the wedding at Cana the party at Cana. And we would not be wrong to do so.

The wedding feast is to be a party and when Jesus asked the attendants to draw out the water, now turned to wine, they knew the party would have no end. The steward was shocked to find not only that the wine was flowing again but that it was the best wine. "The steward called the bridegroom and said to him, 'Everyone serves the good wine first, and then the inferior wine after the guests have become drunk. But you have kept the good wine until now.'" Jesus performed this miracle at Cana "and revealed his glory; and his disciples believed in him."

But it reveals even more for us. The nuptial imagery of Hosea and Isaiah is coming to its fulfillment. The people of God have been called to a party where the best wine never runs out and the "bridegroom rejoices over the bride." The church, the bride of Christ, has been called to a party where "your God rejoices over you." Let's drink to that. With the best wine.

How do you celebrate the wedding feast and experience God's rejoicing over you?

BODY BUILDING

Third Sunday in Ordinary Time

Readings: Neh 8:2-10; Ps 19:8-15;
1 Cor 12:12-30; Luke 1:1-4; 4:14-21

"The joy of the Lord is your strength." (Neh 8:10)

The church is a body of believers, and each part is essential for the overall health of the body. According to St. Paul, each individual person is vital for the body to thrive. All three of the readings for the Third Sunday in Ordinary Time place us in the context of the body of believers. Two of these three passages situate us among the Jewish covenant people. In the first, Ezra reads from the book of the law to the people assembled outside Jerusalem; in the gospel, Jesus reads from the prophets to the people of the synagogue.

Though questions swirl around the historical figure of Ezra, we know that he returned under Persian rule to the land of Judah after the Babylonian destruction and exile to find a people without the word of God. Before the gathered people enter Jerusalem, they ask Ezra to read to them from the law (Neh 7:1-5). When Ezra proclaims the Torah to the people, he not only reads it; he also interprets it. His special task is to bring the word of God to the people, but their task is to hear and accept. They accept the Torah with tears and mourning, but again Ezra acts as their interpreter, telling them to eat, drink, and celebrate "for the joy of the Lord is your strength."

This same communal joy permeates Jesus' reading in Luke 4. Jesus is in his hometown synagogue, an institution whose origin as "village assembly" emerged in the Persian period. Indeed, Anders Runesson, a specialist on the origin of synagogues in early Judaism, links Luke 4 with Nehemiah 8 because the reforms implemented by Ezra and Nehemiah focused on the same unique and defining feature of the synagogue: the "public reading" of the Torah (*The Origins of the Synagogue: A Socio-Historical Study*, ConBNT 37 [Stockholm: Almquist & Wiksell, 2001], 68–69).

Luke, unlike Mark and Matthew, has placed Jesus' reading at the synagogue as the moment in which he begins his ministry, with a spirit-filled public proclamation to his people. But when Jesus reads the Isaian prophecy, a prophecy drenched with good news for the poor and the oppressed, he not only speaks of the promises of God but interprets them, claiming that he is the fulfillment of these hopes and promises. Luke says that "the eyes of all in the synagogue were fixed on him," a description that evokes the people's initial response of wonder: How will Jesus' fulfillment of the word be enacted?

The word was enacted in the church, the body of believers in the Messiah Jesus, who themselves are a part of the mystical Body of Christ. In practice, the church emerged as a type of synagogue structure, a voluntary association based upon the word and person of Jesus. Saint Paul speaks of the "one Spirit" by which "we were all baptized into one body." And yet division seems to suffuse the church in Corinth. Paul insists, amid a world that valued superiority and hierarchy, that every part had its crucial role in the Body of Christ. Paul's desire is that there be "no division in the body, but that the parts may have the same concern for one another. If one part suffers, all the parts suffer with it; if one part is honored, all the parts share its joy." Paul does not deny spiritual gifts or differences among gifts but insists that all are necessary for the body.

All of these passages speak to the need of the people of God to hear and accept the word of God and then to respond to that word with the joy inherent in it, just as Ezra spoke to the people of Jerusalem and Jesus spoke to his neighbors in Nazareth. This is not a passive task, for God's people must go beyond reception of the word to enact the word through the gifts by which each member of the body is graced. "For in the one Spirit we were all baptized into one body—Jews or Greeks, slaves or free—and we were all made to drink of one Spirit. Indeed, the body does not consist of one member but of many." Whatever the role of an individual person within the church, the Body of Christ, each person participates in the priestly, prophetic, and kingly offices of Jesus Christ. In these readings we see the participation of the people of Christ in the prophetic office particularly, called to hear the word as witnesses but also to recognize joyfully our gifts for the evangelization of the world.

Meditate on the words of Scripture. How are you hearing and acting on the word of God in your life?

Love Never Fails

Fourth Sunday in Ordinary Time

Readings: Jer 1:4-19; Ps 71:1-17;
1 Cor 12:31-13:13; Luke 4:21-30

"And I will show you a still more excellent way." (1 Cor 12:31)

Love never fails because God, who is love, never fails. Human loves can be disordered and disintegrate because they can be built upon our own misguided hopes and desires. We mistake what we want or how we perceive something for how things must be or truly are. When Jesus spoke in the synagogue in Nazareth, his initial proclamation was greeted warmly: "All spoke highly of him and were amazed at the gracious words that came from his mouth." Yet when Jesus speaks of God's healing love among the Gentiles, drawing on examples from the prophets Elijah and Elisha, Luke presents a group of people suddenly enraged. How could things change so fast? Luke does not offer us many details, but it seems peoples' expectations regarding God's salvation were not met. Jesus had just spoken of his prophetic fulfillment in the synagogue among his own people, so why would he place God's fulfillment of Israel's hopes among the Gentiles? In addition, something else is bubbling under the surface with respect to Jesus, as to whether he is truly "the one." After all, "Isn't this the son of Joseph?"

The scene Luke sketches, though short and dramatic, encapsulates the human desire to manage and control events. We think we know how things ought to go, and we are often certain we know who people are. We are quick to order the world according to our own wishes and desires. Because of this, the proclamation of the word of God does not always fall on fertile soil. It is not what we wanted, hoped for, or expected. It is too challenging, too generous, or too different. The person God has chosen for a task is not someone who we feel has the proper qualifications.

The prophet Jeremiah had the same doubts about himself. Though the word of God came to Jeremiah saying, "Before I formed you in the womb

I knew you, before you were born I dedicated you, a prophet to the nations I appointed you," he initially rejects his own worthiness for the call. God declares, though, that he will deliver Jeremiah. The psalmist, too, understands that it is God who is his strength: "For you, O Lord, are my hope, my trust, O Lord, from my youth. Upon you I have leaned from my birth; it was you who took me from my mother's womb." Even before we are born we are known to God, called by God and depend upon God even when God's plans are unclear to us.

As creations of God there is something else that binds all of us together, the essence of God himself, which is love. This is why Paul speaks of love as the greatest of spiritual gifts—it is the gift that, unlike prophecy or knowledge, is eternal. More than that, it is the gift that is available to all of us, regardless of our call or understanding. From the aged to the athlete, from those disabled to those just born, love is our heritage. We are worthy of love by the very fact of our creation and being. Ceslas Spicq says that this love, *agape* in the New Testament, is a "demonstration of love," "a divine love, coming from heaven" and a love that "links persons of different conditions: with rulers, benefactors and fathers; it is a disinterested and generous love, full of thoughtfulness and concern. It is in this sense that God is *agape* and loves the world" (*Theological Lexicon of the New Testament, Volume 1* [Peabody, MA: Hendrickson, 1995], 12–13).

It is this outpouring of *agape* that points to the inherent and true value of all human life: we are made to receive God's love and to share God's love. Our blind spots, personal or societal, can blind us to the true meaning and purpose of life. The anger at the Nazareth synagogue emerged from mistaken notions of how God should or must act and led to the rejection of Jesus' proclamation that God's love incarnate in him was for all peoples. God's love is not dependent upon our human calculation of gifts and capabilities. The rejection of the little ones in our society—whether the unborn, the aged, the disabled, or the poor—emerges from our assessment of people as products we can evaluate. But the performance that God desires from us, to which he has called every one of us, is simply this: that we love one another. And this love never fails.

As you reflect on God's greatest gift of love, are you open to this gift in your life and sharing it with others?

THe TransFormers

Readings: Isa 6:1-8; Ps 138:1-8;
1 Cor 15:1-11; Luke 5:1-11

"Go away from me, Lord; for I am a sinful man!" (Luke 5:8)

If God were completely "other," we could not relate to God because God would be different from us in every way. But Genesis assures us that we are made in the image and likeness of God. So even in the matter of holiness there can be some similarity, but God's holiness is so far beyond ours that the encounter of a human being with the living God is powerful and transformative. When the prophet Isaiah envisions God's throne, he hears and sees the seraphs singing, "Holy, holy, holy is the Lord of hosts." Isaiah's initial response to God's holiness is to cry, "Woe is me; I am doomed!" God's holiness, in the form of a burning coal, is placed upon Isaiah's lips; and he is not only purified, but prepared for his call, as his "wickedness is removed" and his "sin purged."

The confrontation with God's holiness has transformed Isaiah; he is now the man who responds to God's call not with shame or fear, but by saying, "Here I am. Send me!"

That same transformative power was operative in Jesus. The Gospel of Luke presents Jesus' call of the first disciples, Simon Peter, James, and John, differently than Mark or Matthew. In the other Synoptic Gospels, there is a simple call and response. In Luke, the call and response are placed in the context of the manifestation of Jesus' power. Luke subtly answers a question that the other two Synoptic Gospels raise in our minds: Why did the disciples respond to Jesus' call so quickly?

Jesus comes among the fisherman not in some "holy" or otherworldly setting, but in their day-to-day work lives—at the shore while they are cleaning their nets. After Simon, James, and John had a night of unfruitful fishing, Jesus instructs Simon to "put out into deep water and lower your nets for a catch." Simon counters by telling Jesus that their hard work has not been rewarded all night, "but at your command I will lower the nets." This act of faith is rewarded with overflowing nets and boats sinking under the weight of the catch. Simon knows that it is Jesus who has brought them this catch and recognizes in him the awful power of God. As with the prophet Isaiah, the presence of the divine overwhelms Simon and illuminates his weakness and sinfulness. His cry, so similar to Isaiah, is "Depart from me, Lord, for I am a sinful man."

Yet the presence of God in our lives not only illuminates our weakness, but strengthens and emboldens us as it transforms us. Jesus simply instructs Simon not to be afraid. Simon and the others clearly hear the call, for the disciples "left everything and followed him." It is that same powerful presence of Jesus Christ that was revealed to Paul and transformed him from persecutor to evangelist. Indeed, in 1 Corinthians 15, Paul speaks of the reality of Jesus Christ and encapsulates his transformation in what is perhaps the earliest Christian creed: "For I handed on to you as of first importance what I also received: that Christ died for our sins in accordance with the Scriptures; that he was buried; that he was raised on the third day in accordance with the Scriptures; that he appeared to Cephas, then to the Twelve."

This proto-creed is not intended to be a dry summation of realities long gone and fondly remembered, but a sign of God's power and reality still active. For the same God who came to Isaiah, Simon Peter, and Paul is still calling us in the church and beyond to encounter the living God, to be purified by his cleansing power, to cast off fear and to respond to the call to be transformed by God's grace. And it is still the case that God's call comes to us and meets us where we are in the world, whether called like Isaiah to encounter God in his glory or like Peter to meet God as he performed his daily tasks. The message in every case is clear: Do not be afraid to encounter God's holiness—it will burn off our fear and reveal the holiness for which God has created us.

God's "otherness" is not intended to drive us away from him but to draw us near to him. It is when we respond to God's call that we can call out to God confidently with the psalmist: "When I called, you answered me; you built up strength within me."

Place yourself in the presence of God with Peter and the other disciples. Can you accept God coming near to you?

THe DeaD WILL LIVe

Sixth Sunday in Ordinary Time

Readings: Jer 17:5-8; Ps 1:1-4, 6;
1 Cor 15:12-20; Luke 6:17-26

*"Now if Christ is proclaimed as raised from the dead, how can some
of you say there is no resurrection of the dead?"* (1 Cor 15:12)

Part of what may cause problems in accepting the reality of the general
resurrection of the dead, both in first-century Corinth and twenty-first-
century Minneapolis, for example, is that even if one proclaims Christ as
raised from the dead, where are the other examples? People might be
willing to take solace in the claims of resurrection as a metaphor, or a kind
of shared memory of a loved one, but most often when Christians go
astray on this teaching of the church it is in a way that does not deny the
resurrection so much as overlook its full meaning.

The reality of Christ's resurrection from the dead and subsequent ascension led to the belief, embedded in the Creed, that Jesus "will come
again in glory / to judge the living and the dead / and his kingdom will
have no end." It also proclaims, at the end of the Creed, that we "look
forward to the resurrection of the dead / and the life of the world to come."
But it is the interim period that was created by Christ's resurrection and
ascension that also led to a greater focus on what happened to those who
died prior to Christ's return. Did they exist even now? If so, how did they
exist? And where were they?

Jews prior to the Christians had contemplated the place of the dead
before the general resurrection and they had speculated that there was an
abode for all of the dead, Sheol, but increasingly wondered whether there
were places of punishment and reward even prior to the resurrection. For
Paul, the question of what happened to the dead prior to Christ's return
probably arose in equal measure from his Pharisaic theological education,
practical considerations of Christians who had died prior to Christ's return, and simple reflection on Christ's continuing existence even now with

God. In Philippians 1:21-23, Paul muses on whether he will survive his Roman imprisonment, claiming that "to me, living is Christ and dying is gain. If I am to live in the flesh, that means fruitful labor for me; and I do not know which I prefer. I am hard pressed between the two: my desire is to depart and be with Christ, for that is far better." In that claim, that to depart this world is to "be with Christ" we find an early claim about Christian hope for the dead prior to the resurrection. The text of Philippians supports an intermediate state between living in the body here on earth and the resurrection at the end of time, a state that we generally refer to as heaven, but also includes the possibilities of purgatory and hell.

Paul repeats this claim about an intermediate period in 2 Corinthians 5, where he outlines three human states of life: those who are living here on earth; the "naked" (*gymnos* = disembodied = dead), those who are "unclothed" and "away from the body and at home with the Lord"; and the "further clothed" (= resurrection/transformation at the Parousia), which Paul also calls living in "a house made by God." When Paul considers these three states, Paul prefers the "further clothed" or resurrected state to *gymnos* (= death) or being "away from the body and at home with the Lord" (2 Cor 5:2-5). But in 2 Corinthians 5:6-9, Paul finds that to be "away from the body" and "with the Lord" is preferable to this world. The *Catechism of the Catholic Church* comments on this passage, especially 2 Corinthians 5:8, saying, "to rise with Christ, we must die with Christ: we must 'be away from the body and at home with the Lord.' In that 'departure' which is death the soul is separated from the body. It will be reunited with the body on the day of the resurrection of the dead" (1005).

And that is the ultimate hope: the resurrection of the dead. It is not that heaven, life in the presence of God, is not wonderful; it is that we have been created by God, body and soul, to spend our lives in the kingdom of God, not as disembodied souls, but as whole people, created to become more like God in every way. Paul tells us that our faith hinges on this, for "If Christ has not been raised, your faith is futile and you are still in your sins," but Paul promises "Christ has been raised from the dead, the first fruits of those who have died." And Christ, the firstfruits, is the promise of the harvest, the resurrection, of all who have died with him.

Pray with Paul's passages on the resurrection. Do you have questions about the resurrection of the dead?

THE SPIRITUAL BODY

Seventh Sunday in Ordinary Time

Readings: 1 Sam 26:2-23; Ps 103:1-13;
1 Cor 15:45-49; Luke 6:27-38

"We will also bear the image of the man of heaven." (1 Cor 15:49)

"How does Paul know all of this?," a bewildered student asked me in class one day when we were reading 1 Corinthians 15. The passages on the resurrection and the resurrection body, which Paul details in 1 Corinthians 15, speak of realities we have not experienced and cannot by reason alone establish. So, how does Paul know all of this? The short answer is revelation; the slightly longer answer includes the tradition of the early church, some of whose members witnessed the resurrected Jesus, Jewish theology of the first century, and Paul's own mystical experiences, detailed in 2 Corinthians 12.

Paul writes that all will be resurrected on the last day, when death is conquered and life reigns supreme eternally. Paul assumes that when we are resurrected we will receive a spiritual body, and that the body we have here on earth, our physical body, must be transformed before we can enter the kingdom of God, for "flesh and blood cannot inherit the kingdom of God" (1 Cor 15:50). This is powerful and revelatory writing, but so important for disciples of Jesus because it points to our true destiny. And our true destiny includes our bodies.

This is significant because of the many ways in which we treat our bodies or the bodies of others, sometimes with disdain or even hatred, sometimes with shame and disregard, and sometimes, it is true, with love and care. It is not wrong to want to live healthy lives and care for our bodies, yet even this can lead to body image issues, as we strive to meet unattainable ideals or shape our bodies into what we think is the perfect body. Others treat their bodies as insignificant vessels and treat them with hatred or are unable to see them truly, only seeing faults and imperfections.

We need to see our bodies as what they are intended to be: a part of whole human persons who are loved by God for who we are and as we are. Paul actually takes us back to the creation account in Genesis 2:7 when he speaks of the human body, writing, "the first man, Adam, became a living being." This man, says Paul, was physical, "from the earth, a man of dust," and so are we all: living, physical beings. In this creation account, when the man and woman are cast out of the Garden after their fall one of the consequences of the fall is that they "knew that they were naked." There is an element of sexual shame that is often tied to interpretations of this passage, but it might also be that their physicality itself, the very bodies that they took for granted, is now subject to critical judgment and shame.

Our bodies are a sign of our uniqueness, intended to speak to our continuation in the world to come as individuals not drops in the ocean swallowed up by the oneness of all things. And as we believe we will be perfected in the world to come, so Paul says our physicality, too, will be transformed and brought to fulfillment. For as "the first man was from the earth, a man of dust," Adam, so "the second man is from heaven," Jesus. Paul uses here a first Adam, second Adam typology that he uses in other of his letters.

Jesus was obedient to God in all things and so "the last Adam," Jesus, "became a life-giving spirit." But it is not that Jesus himself is *just* a spiritual being. Jesus, too, in his resurrected body continues to exist in the transformed, resurrected body. But as "the first man was from the earth, a man of dust; the second man is from heaven. As was the man of dust, so are those who are of the dust; and as is the man of heaven, so are those who are of heaven." The purpose of the resurrection is that our bodies will be transformed into *spiritual*, perfected, bodies, something congruous with who we are, but different than what we were. Paul explains that "just as we have borne the image of the man of dust, we will also bear the image of the man of heaven." And it is this "image of the man of heaven" for which God has intended us. We are to be brought to our true destiny not just through the perfection of our souls but the perfection of our bodies. As we struggle here on earth with moral challenges, so, too, we struggle with our physical challenges, whether bodies we do not like, or limitations of our bodies, but they too have been created by God, intended for transformation in the world to come, loved by God as an integral part of who we are.

Do you struggle with accepting your body today or with the hope of the resurrected body?

Death Loses

Eighth Sunday in Ordinary Time

Readings: Isa 55:10-13; Ps 92:1-15;
1 Cor 15:51-58; Luke 6:39-49

"We will not all die, but we will all be changed." (1 Cor 15:51)

Death is frightening. Most of us hope that it will wait awhile before taking us from the lives we love, ensconced in the comforting presence of our families and friends. It is frightening in large measure because it is the great unknown, even though Scripture tells us it has been conquered and even though we might indeed believe intellectually that it has been conquered. At some visceral level, though, because of the finality of death and the tangible reality that, with one glaring exception, dead people do not rise from the dead, we often dread death and the ultimate change it bears with it. We fear the loss of the life we know so well.

The first-century churches to which Paul wrote had the same issues with accepting death that we have today, in terms of dread and fright, but they also had a difficult time understanding the new concept known as resurrection. Those Christians who were Greek or Roman had mostly hoped for the continuation of the immortal soul as their final destiny prior to the Christian gospel being preached to them. The body was often seen as a sort of prison house that they would be happy to slough off when their time on earth was done; they would hope for a good eternity, but for the soul alone. The resurrection that Paul preached in Corinth, however, is much more than immortality of the soul; it is the rising from the dead of the transformed person, body and soul.

Before examining the physical nature of the resurrected person, Paul says an interesting thing that he calls a "mystery": "We will not all die, but we will all be changed, in a moment, in the twinkling of an eye, at the last trumpet." The sound of the trumpet is an ancient apocalyptic image of the impending judgment, but what does Paul mean when he says "we will not all die"? Paul is saying that both those who have died prior to the

Last Judgment and those who are alive at the coming of Christ must be *changed* (*allassô*). This verb has the sense of exchanging one thing for another, or transforming something, and it is this "change" that Paul designates as the *mystery*, or "secret." While our eternal existence will indeed be embodied, it is not the physical body (*sôma phsyikon*) we have here on earth, but a spiritual body (*sôma pneumatikon*), a "changed" body, that will inherit the kingdom of God.

At the eschaton, "the trumpet will sound, and the dead will be raised imperishable, and we will be changed. For this perishable body must put on imperishability, and this mortal body must put on immortality." In 1 Corinthians 15:50, Paul called those who are still alive at the coming of Christ "flesh and blood" and those who are still "flesh and blood" at the coming of Christ will see their mortal bodies "put on immortality," while those who have already died "must put on imperishability." What is translated as "the perishable body" (*to phthartos*) actually does not refer to something that *might* perish, but something that has already experienced corruption and decay, that is, those who have already died. Paul's claim is that to inherit the kingdom of God both the living and the dead must both be transformed. It is not that there will be no corporeal participation in the resurrection, but that each body, living or dead, must be transformed into a resurrection body.

Death is real, Paul says, but it is also something that he elsewhere refers to as being "asleep," since it is not the final word. God is the God of the living, not the dead. And while we might indeed fear death at the darkest moments of our lives or separation from our loved ones forever, we fear death precisely because it is not what God intended for humanity or his creation. Corruption, decay, and death are interlopers in God's good creation, for we have been made for eternity. And so Paul offers this insight, "when those who are dead put on imperishability, and those who are liable to death put on immortality, then the saying that is written will be fulfilled: 'Death has been swallowed up in victory.' 'Where, O death, is your victory? Where, O death, is your sting?' " This is the victory, indeed, which is prefigured in the resurrection of Christ, the victory for which he gave his own life in order that we might all be like him and live for eternity with God, perfected in body and soul.

Meditate on these verses from 1 Corinthians 15. Do you fear death? How do these verses comfort you as you reflect on death?

servants and slaves

Ninth Sunday in Ordinary Time

Readings: 1 Kgs 8:22-23, 41-43; Ps 96:1-9;
Gal 1:1-12; Luke 7:1-10

*"If I were still pleasing people, I would not
be a servant of Christ."* (Gal 1:10)

The ancient world was populated by people who were servants and slaves. Parsing the differences between servants and slaves in antiquity is complex and technical work, yet we can say that there was a range of formal servitude in which people were subject to others, but not considered their property, or owned by others and legally considered as belonging to their masters, who could basically dispense with them as they chose. In the gospel passage from Luke, the complexities of servitude, according to Roman law, the politics of colonialism, military command, and the true authority of God, are all on display.

In the account in Luke 7, a Roman centurion who was stationed in Capernaum had a slave (*doulos*) who was ill, and he sent some Jewish elders on his behalf to inquire whether Jesus might heal him. The man with military, political, and legal authority here is the centurion, for he commanded soldiers, slaves, and the Jewish elders, since the Romans at the time of Jesus governed Judea and the whole region of Syria. He might have exercised his authority over all of these parties as a petty tyrant, throwing his weight around to get his way.

But early on in the account, we learn that the slave was "valued highly." While that might mean the slave was simply considered a valuable piece of property, the Greek word used, *entimos*, has more of a sense of someone who is held in honor or considered precious. It seems as if the centurion cared for his ill slave as a human being. We also learn that the Jewish elders have not taken on the task to seek out Jesus as cowed colonial subjects, but because he has been a friend of the Jewish people and someone who respects God. They advise Jesus, "he is worthy of having you do this for him, for he loves our people, and it is he who built our synagogue for us."

Jesus accompanies the Jewish elders to the home of the centurion to heal the slave. Yet before Jesus arrived at his house, friends of the centurion were sent to tell Jesus, "Lord, do not trouble yourself, for I am not worthy to have you come under my roof; therefore I did not presume to come to you. But only speak the word, and let my servant be healed." We note here that the centurion to this point has only sent emissaries to represent his authority: what he asks and says has been done. He has sent for Jesus precisely because he does not have the authority to heal his beloved slave, but he trusts that Jesus has this power and authority.

And we know that his slave is beloved for in his message to Jesus he calls him, literally, "my child." It is true that *pais*, "child" in Greek, might also be used as a circumlocution for "slave," but it is also possible that his close relationship to his slave is on display here. The centurion has a proper grasp of the limits of his power, both in terms of how he treats those under his authority, but also in recognizing his own limitations. He can tell a soldier, "Go," and he goes, and to another, "Come," and he comes, and to my slave, "Do this," and the slave does it. When it comes to the spiritual power of God, however, he has aligned himself with the God of the Jews, and knows that it is Jesus who represents God's authority. The centurion has properly placed his faith in Jesus as the true representative of God.

The centurion has faith not only that Jesus has the power to heal his slave, but that he will do this on behalf even of a Gentile soldier who occupies his nation. Jesus' identification of the centurion's faith—"I tell you, not even in Israel have I found such faith"—tells us that faith resides in both Jew and Gentile. It also tells us that the centurion understood that true authority and power are from God, and God's authority transcends the artificial divisions that humans establish between themselves as slaves and commanders or Jews and Gentiles. God has authority over all of us. This is why Paul identifies himself in Galatians as a *doulos* of Christ, which literally means "slave," and why King Solomon calls himself an *ebed* of God, which might be translated as "servant" or in some contexts "slave." We are all, whether centurion, apostle, or king, subject to the authority of the one, true God.

Reflect on the centurion's response to Jesus. How do you acknowledge the power and authority of God?

RISE UP!

Tenth Sunday in Ordinary Time

Readings: 1 Kgs 17:17-24; Ps 30:2-13;
Gal 1:11-19; Luke 7:11-17

"When the Lord saw her, he had compassion for her." (Luke 7:13)

The prophet Elijah "went to Zarephath of Sidon to the house of a widow." While Elijah was at the widow's home, her son died. Already bereft of a husband, which itself often led women into poverty in the ancient world, she has now lost her son, the remaining source of her emotional and economic sustenance. She turns on Elijah, "Why have you done this to me, O man of God? Have you come to me to call attention to my guilt and to kill my son?" Elijah does not defend himself or declare his innocence, but responds directly to the pain and loss underlying her accusation. He responds, that is, with compassion.

Surprisingly, perhaps, Elijah aligns himself with the Gentile widow as he cries out to God, "O Lord, my God, will you afflict even the widow with whom I am staying by killing her son?" He continues to pray, "O Lord, my God, let the life breath return to the body of this child." God hears Elijah's prayer, and life returns to the boy. When Elijah returned the child alive to his widowed mother, she said to him, "Now indeed I know that you are a man of God. The word of the Lord comes truly from your mouth."

This act of mercy and compassion, returning a child to his mother, becomes a model for Jesus in his own teaching and healing. Jesus referred to this scene when he spoke in the synagogue in Nazareth (Luke 4). The needs of the suffering outsider were a model for Jesus' own ministry, and not just in speech and archetype. In the gospel passage Jesus comes across a situation very similar in character to that which Elijah faced.

In the town of Nain, Jesus witnessed a funeral procession, with a widow mourning her only son. Jesus is moved with compassion by her suffering, a compassion expressed with the Greek verb *splanchnizomai*. The verb evokes Jesus' emotional response by expressing the kind of deep physical experience that often accompanies empathy. He is moved "in his bowels," thought then to be the location of the emotions of pity and love. He instructs her, "Do not cry!" This command becomes Jesus' word that he will bring relief to the bereaved widow. Jesus goes directly to the coffin and, touching it, speaks: "Young man, I tell you, arise!" When the young man sat up, "Jesus gave him to his mother."

Just as the widow at Zarephath recognized God at work through Elijah, the people who witnessed Jesus' action declare that "God has visited his people." God's power at work in Jesus' action also points beyond itself and foreshadows another mother and only son, who in his death would leave her bereft but in his return would increase the joy not only of her but of all his followers, no longer bearers in a mournful funeral procession but brought to new life. But as with Elijah's act, what Jesus performs is also concrete help for those who are weak and vulnerable. Jesus' action at this level is not so much the fulfillment of a messianic type, but a copy of how God has always acted on behalf of those most in need. God brings unexpected life to the sons of widows because God is for the least among us.

It is certainly the case, though, that unlike Elijah and Jesus, we do not bring to life the dead sons of mourning widows. Still, these stories point us to the type of person Christians are called to be. Like Jesus, we are all capable of performing acts of mercy and compassion for those in need. Our culture might hold up as ideals power, control, and strength, especially for men, but at the heart of Jesus' strength is compassion for weakness, mercy for the helpless. The person who acts against the victimization of women, the proliferation of pornography, the scourge of human trafficking, and slavery is acting like Elijah and Jesus with compassion and mercy. Those women and children released from poverty and sufferings share in some part the resurrection of Jesus in the world. This is a model for us, the type of people Jesus calls us to be for those in need.

Reflect on the mercy and compassion of Jesus. Where am I witnessing the sufferings of our world and how can I best respond to those in need?

A WOMAN BELOVED BY GOD

Eleventh Sunday in Ordinary Time

Readings: 2 Sam 12:7-13; Ps 32:1-11;
Gal 2:16-21; Luke 7:36–8:3

"Your faith has saved you; go in peace." (Luke 7:50)

Jesus' love for the weak and marginalized is made manifest in a powerful account in Luke's gospel, as is the human willingness to label and disenfranchise people we consider less worthy. In today's narrative, Jesus suggests that we start to identify who we truly are in relationship not to social standards but to God's overwhelming love. Jesus is invited to eat at the home of a Pharisee named Simon. His identity is clear: Simon, the Pharisee. But a woman, who remains nameless, operating on the assumption that well-behaved women rarely meet the Messiah, hears of Jesus' presence in the house and crashes the dinner party. Her identity is also clear: "a woman in the city, who was a sinner."

When this woman found Jesus, she treated him with honor and love: "She stood behind him at his feet, weeping, and began to bathe his feet with her tears and to dry them with her hair. Then she continued kissing his feet and anointing them with the ointment." Simon's response to these demonstrations of affection and love emerge in the context of his understanding of how people should act: "If this man were a prophet, he would have known who and what kind of woman this is who is touching him— that she is a sinner." A prophet, clearly, should not allow a "sinner," especially a woman, to touch him; and a woman, a notorious sinner, should not touch a prophet. Everyone knows that.

Jesus responds by telling Simon a story of two debtors, one of whom owed the creditor five hundred denarii and the other fifty. Seeing that they were unable to pay their debts, the creditor decided to cancel the debts of both debtors. Jesus asks Simon, "Now which of them will love him more?" Simon answers by saying that the one with the greater debt will love the creditor more, and Jesus agrees with him. The meaning of this simple story for Simon, the woman, and Jesus will soon become clear. It depends upon a correct identification of the creditor and the two debtors.

Jesus explains the story by describing the love the unnamed woman poured out on Jesus, by washing and kissing his feet and anointing his head with oil, which stands in stark contrast to Simon's diffidence to Jesus. Jesus says, "I tell you, her sins, which were many, have been forgiven; hence she has shown great love. But the one to whom little is forgiven, loves little. Then he said to her, 'Your sins are forgiven.' " It is with Jesus' claim that her sins were forgiven that Simon's friends began to question Jesus and to ask each other, "Who is this who even forgives sins?"

It is the answer to this question, however, that allows the proper identification of all parties in this scenario. Jesus does not deny that the woman is a sinner—she is the one with the greater debt than Simon in Jesus' parable—but she has correctly identified Jesus as the one who is able to forgive her sins. That is, Jesus is her creditor. She pours out her love on Jesus in thanksgiving for the forgiveness of her sins and in acknowledgment of his messiahship, expressed especially when she anoints Jesus with oil; she recognizes that he is the one with the authority to wipe away her debt. As a result, Jesus can say to her, "Your faith has saved you; go in peace."

But Simon is unable either to see himself as a debtor—that is, a sinner—or Jesus as the one who is willing and able to forgive sins. Jesus agrees with the identification of the woman as a sinner, but what Simon does not recognize is that he, too, is a sinner, even if his debt is lighter. Unless Simon can see himself as "the sinful man" and acknowledge his debt, he cannot be forgiven. Unless he identifies Jesus as the one who can forgive his debt, he cannot turn to him in love and repent.

Yes, the woman is a sinner, but so are we all. Simon judges her on human terms, but we need the ability to identify her as God sees her, known by name and beloved by God, and to recognize in ourselves the need for God's healing forgiveness regardless of our names or positions.

Imagine yourself in Simon's house. When you hear Jesus tell the story, do you identify with the woman who is a sinner or Simon?

The One I Look For

Twelfth Sunday in Ordinary Time

Readings: Zech 12:10-11; 13:1; Ps 63:2-9;
Gal 3:26-29; Luke 9:18-24

"But who do you say that I am?" (Luke 9:20)

Years ago the band U2 recorded "I Still Haven't Found What I'm Looking For." Could Jesus' first disciples have said that? To know what you are looking for, you have to know what you need. When you know what you need, you need to know where to look for it in order to identify it. Was he the one they were looking for? Was he the Messiah, the one who was to come? If it seems obvious to us today, we need to put ourselves in the sandals of the first-century Jews.

Christians read the Old Testament now in the light of Jesus' words and deeds, especially the complex of events encompassing his death, resurrection, and ascension. Christians read the Old Testament today inspired by the Holy Spirit, who would come, the Gospel of John says, and guide them into all truth. Clearly Peter, James, John, Mary Magdalene, Joanna, and Susanna, among many others, would not have followed Jesus if they were not attracted by his teaching and person, but was he the Messiah? They would have read the Torah and Prophets and wondered about passages like Zechariah 12:10, where we read that God "will pour out a spirit of compassion and supplication on the house of David and the inhabitants of Jerusalem, so that, when they look on the one whom they have pierced, they shall mourn for him, as one mourns for an only child, and weep bitterly over him, as one weeps over a firstborn." At the time of Jesus' mission along the dusty streets of Galilee, Samaria, and Judea, who among Jesus' disciples could have predicted that this would refer to Jesus? How could they know "the one whom they have pierced" referred to the Messiah? And did they know Jesus was the Messiah?

It was only toward the end of Jesus' ministry, when, Luke tells us, he had "set his face to go to Jerusalem" (9:51), that he begins to unravel a bit further the mystery that is his life, a destiny hidden in his teachings and the Scriptures. After feeding the crowds by the miraculous multiplication of fish and loaves, Jesus is alone praying, with only his closest disciples nearby. He asks them a question: "Who do the crowds say that I am?" They all have answers ready, offering that the crowds have proclaimed him John the Baptist, Elijah, and even "one of the ancient prophets." Jesus then asks them the harder question, the personal question, "But who do you say that I am?"

Again, an answer is ready, and unsurprisingly, it is Peter who responds, "The Christ of God." Jesus' response to this answer has always been puzzling to readers, for Jesus "rebuked them" (plural in Luke, which indicates that all the apostles shared this view, not just Peter) "and directed them not to tell this to anyone." The puzzle is this: Why would the Messiah, who has called people to follow him, whose goal is to establish the kingdom of God, which by definition requires that there be subjects of the king, not want it known that he is the king? In the scholarly world, this mystery has come to be known as "the messianic secret." Scholars wonder whether this was a literary construction of the gospel authors, either as an explanation of why Jesus' messianic claims were not acknowledged or as a retrojection of later Christian messianic claims. I offer Jesus' answer instead: "The Son of Man must suffer greatly and be rejected by the elders, the chief priests, and the scribes, and be killed and on the third day be raised."

How does this scenario answer the question, "But who do you say I am?" It does so by reorienting the answer from an identification rife with expectations of messianic glory and triumph to those of the messiah Jesus was and would be, namely, a messiah who would suffer and die on behalf of humanity and who would ask each follower to "deny himself and take up his cross daily and follow me." Jesus is asking his apostles not just to identify the Messiah but in identifying the Messiah to accept the destiny of "the one whom they have pierced" as God's plan for Jesus, the one they were looking for.

Reflect on Jesus' question, "But who do you say that I am?" Have you found the one you were looking for, and are you willing to share his destiny?

Prophetic Values

Thirteenth Sunday in Ordinary Time

Readings: 1 Kgs 19:16-21; Ps 16:1-11;
Gal 5:1, 13-18; Luke 9:51-62

"I will follow you wherever you go." (Luke 9:57)

The language of the Bible can be gently potent. Biblical texts are not usually wordy, nor do biblical characters elaborate their feelings in lengthy soliloquies. A few words are offered to be pondered, measured, and considered. People speak directly, but sometimes the meaning is mysterious or opposed to closely held expectations of how God ought to act or what God's spokespeople ought to say. Before jettisoning the peculiarity of God's ways or the idiosyncrasies of God's representatives, we ought to consider why God speaks to us in this way. If hard or direct words evoke discomfort, what is God telling us and what do we need to hear?

When the prophet Elijah came to anoint Elisha to take his place as God's prophet, Elisha was plowing with twelve oxen. Elijah called him by placing his cloak over Elisha's shoulders, a symbolic action signifying his prophetic call and an action that Elisha understood. Elisha seems not to reject the call, but says to Elijah, "Let me kiss my father and my mother, and then I will follow you." Elijah responds to this seemingly innocent request with what appears to be a sharp rejection, "Go back again; for what have I done to you?"

How does a newly anointed prophet respond to Elijah's question, "for what have I done to you?" It is not clear if (1) Elijah is telling Elisha to "go back" on his prophetically chosen mission—that is, reject what God has instructed him to do through Elijah, if Elisha is not prepared to leave immediately or (2) Elijah is telling Elisha that nothing has been done to him if he cannot respond to the call without turning back to his family, if only for a moment.

Either way, prophetic values trump family values for Elisha, as he slaughters his animals, cooks them over his burning plows, and feeds his people before leaving with Elijah. There can be no clearer statement of the rejection of his past life than his burning up his livelihood and feeding it to others. I interpret Elijah's words to Elisha in this way: Keep doing what you do or start doing what God has called you to do, but you can't do both; so make a decision.

It is for this same reason that Jesus rejects the question asked by James and John, when the Samaritan village they passed through ignores Jesus' call: "Lord, do you want us to command fire to come down from heaven and consume them?" It is a startling human reaction by the Sons of Thunder—you have snubbed the Messiah; now face a fiery punishment—but Jesus rebukes them and their desired payback for the perceived slight. There is no point in crushing the Samaritans for the choice they made. They have chosen to keep doing what they do and there is no point in seeking vengeance. They are, like all of us, ultimately answerable for their choices and there is no way to know if it will be their final choice.

The Samaritans in Luke's scene simply do not follow, but many others claim that they will follow Jesus wherever he goes, but when profound human and familial needs arise, they are torn. The choice to follow is put on hold, while human calculations are made. It is not that these concerns are minor—"Lord, first let me go and bury my father" is a major act of filial devotion—it is that God's call is preeminent over all things and at all times. To the would-be follower who says, "I will follow you, Lord; but let me first say farewell to those at my home," Jesus, reformulating Elijah's question to Elisha, says, "No one who puts a hand to the plow and looks back is fit for the kingdom of God."

These are not easy sayings; and if the hardness of them has been lost to us, it may be because we have been too focused on making the hard words of the Bible soft and comfortable. Jesus announces that the call takes precedence not just over our leisure and amusements but our families and professions: Will you follow or will you not? It is a daily choice, perhaps more realistically a constant choice, as to what we decide to do, whether we follow or turn back to our plows. And if we turn back, we must choose to return to the comfort of work and family or to burn our plows and leave.

Imagine yourself with Jesus and his apostles with a crowd in an ancient marketplace. Jesus challenges people in the crowd to follow him. What is holding you back right now from following him?

THE JOY OF JUDGMENT

Fourteenth Sunday in Ordinary Time

Readings: Isa 66:10-14; Ps 66:1-20;
Gal 6:14-18; Luke 10:1-20

"As a mother comforts her child, so will I comfort you." (Isa 66:13)

The English word "crisis" originates with the Greek noun *krisis*, which is itself a derivative of the verb *krinô*, "to judge." A crisis is a time of decision, encapsulating danger and opportunity in equal parts; and the biblical eschaton, the time of God's judgment, is grounded upon the judgments or decisions we have taken throughout our lives. We must all navigate the dangers and opportunities found in the many crises we will all face.

It is in the midst of an eschatological scenario in the book of Isaiah, chapter 66, that the writer known as Third Isaiah presents the image of God as a mother comforting her child. It is not the most common biblical image of God nor the one most commonly associated with the crisis at the end of the world, but it is important, as it presents God as the one who, like our own mothers, desires our comfort, security, and joy.

As with our earthly mothers, though, there is a time when we must make our own judgments about the paths we take, the mistakes we make, and the dangers of our choices. We leave our mothers and the danger is present, but so, too, are the opportunities and the necessity to grow and develop. What we cannot get on an earthly level, however, is a promise of success or comfort and certainly not eternal joy on the basis of our judgments, no matter how well we plan our lives and dance around the dangers. This never-ending joy is something that only God can offer.

It is precisely to make this joyful offer that Jesus sends out seventy emissaries, recalling the seventy elders chosen to be with Moses (Exod 24:1 and 9), to announce the coming kingdom of God. The sending evokes the practical need to share the ministry and the completeness indicated by the number seventy, but Jesus himself alerts us that it is a time of crisis. He notes both the opportunity for those who share in his ministry—"The harvest is plentiful, but the laborers are few"—and the danger for those who have been sent out to join in Jesus' mission—"See, I am sending you out like lambs into the midst of wolves." Yet these dangers represent momentary and passing afflictions when compared to the eternal joy of the kingdom. The weight of the crisis, this time of decision and judgment, is borne by all those who hear the call and who must still decide. The pressing nature of the coming end, when new creation will be the ground of existence in each of us and for each of us, is felt in this passage. Jesus says that those who reject the pronouncement that "the kingdom of God has come near to you" will find on the Day of Judgment that "it will be more tolerable for Sodom than for that town."

While the accent in eschatological scenarios tends not to fall on the note of joy but rather on the consequences for those who reject the call and turn away from the opportunity; it is hope that undergirds Jesus' ministry and pronouncement of the kingdom of God. The seventy, after all, do not return downtrodden after passing on the message of Jesus; they return with joy. It is true that part of their joy rests on their newfound power, but at least some of it must rest on the success they have had in bringing Jesus' message to the surrounding towns and the positive responses they have received. And if that is not where their joy rests, Jesus sets them straight: "Do not rejoice at this, that the spirits submit to you, but rejoice that your names are written in heaven."

This is the true source of joy, of having traversed the dangers of this world like a lamb among wolves, and taken the opportunity to bring God's joy and hope to those around us so that our and their choices lead us to our eternal home. There are numerous crises that we face, time after time when decisions must be made, when judgments must be offered about the choices put before us. The great judgment is intended to be the summation of joy, like a child running home when she hears her mother's voice, safe and secure, comforted in her arms for eternity.

Place yourself among the seventy disciples sent by Jesus to bring the message to the people. What is Jesus calling you to tell the people about the kingdom of God?

PUT IT On MY ACCOUNT

Fifteenth Sunday in Ordinary Time

Readings: Deut 30:10-14; Ps 69:14-37 or
Ps 19:8-11; Col 1:15-20; Luke 10:25-37

"Go and do likewise." (Luke 10:37)

The Christian relationship to the law of Moses is complicated, particularly in light of what the apostle Paul said about the law in his letters. But Paul understood that the law's origin lay with God and that it was not insignificant but rather was fulfilled through Christ Jesus, "the image of the invisible God, the firstborn of all creation." Moses said that the law was the equivalent of hearing "the voice of the Lord, your God" and that the law "is something very near to you, already in your mouths and in your hearts; you have only to carry it out." Since "in him all the fullness was pleased to dwell"—a shorthand way to speak of Jesus' divinity—the fullness of the law and its intentions rested with Jesus and in him.

When a scholar of the law asked Jesus, "Teacher, what must I do to inherit eternal life?" it is not surprising that Jesus asked him in reply: "What is written in the law? How do you read it?" This is not a pop quiz that Jesus sprang on the lawyer, but a question that has to do with the foundation of a well-lived Jewish life. The scholar replied with a portion of the Shema, which remains a basic prayer for Jews today, based on Deuteronomy 6:4-9; 11:13-21 and Numbers 15:37-41. What the lawyer recites in Luke's account is a variation of Deuteronomy 6:5: "You shall love the Lord, your God, with all your heart, with all your being, with all your strength, and with all your mind," combined with Leviticus 19:18, "and your neighbor as yourself." Jesus' response to the lawyer is direct: "You have answered correctly; do this and you will live."

This is not the end of the matter, however, since the scholar, as scholars often do, wants to have the last word. He has a final question: "And who is my neighbor?" Whether the scholar's intentions were true, his question gives us one of the best and certainly the best known of Jesus' parables.

The parable has so many profound spiritual levels that this simple story has taken pages, even books, to unravel it all, but let the focus fall on what it means to follow the law and who is able to follow the law in Jesus' story.

In the account there is a beaten man, half dead, who is ignored and passed by both a priest and Levite who appear to be going to the temple. It is possible they pass the traveler by because they consider him already dead and do not want to place themselves in a state of corpse impurity, which would render their temple service impossible. Maybe they are just concerned with the fact that if the robbers beat one man to death, they might be looking for more victims.

It is the Samaritan, representing a group at odds with the Jews both religiously and politically, who puts aside all concerns for his well-being and acts out of compassion for the victim. Van Gogh's famous painting of this scene moves us with its depiction of the strain on the Samaritan's face as he hoists the beaten man onto his horse, having already cleansed and purified his wounds with oil and wine and bandaged them.

The Samaritan, however, does even more. He takes the victim to an inn and gives two denarii to the innkeeper, money out of his own pocket, and does not stop there: "Take care of him. If you spend more than what I have given you, I shall repay you on my way back." The Samaritan not only opens his wallet but leaves his credit card number behind. His actions say, "Put it on my account."

"And who is my neighbor?" Jesus answers the question, as he so often does, with a question: "Which of these three, in your opinion, was neighbor to the robbers' victim?" In answering Jesus' question, though, the scholar answers his own question. The one who acted like a neighbor was the foreigner, maligned by those around him, and in so doing he identified anyone in need as a neighbor. Jesus' instructions to "go and do likewise" place the fulfillment of the law where it was always intended to be: in love of God and neighbor. As Moses said, "you have only to carry it out."

Reflect on this parable, while imagining yourself walking down a road in your town. Who is the neighbor you are being asked to serve?

AT Your Service

Sixteenth Sunday in Ordinary Time

Readings: Gen 18:1-10; Ps 15:2-5;
Col 1:24-28; Luke 10:38-42

*"My lord, if I find favor with you, do not
pass by your servant."* (Gen 18:3)

There is something charming about the account of Abraham serving the three men who suddenly appear at the oaks of Mamre. It is not simply that Abraham offers unbidden hospitality and service, or that they respond to his offer of food with a simple, "Do as you have said," but that along with the water, bread, curds, and milk he also proffers a tender, young calf to eat. The charm is not in the offer itself. Even a city boy knows that though Abraham has given the calf to his servant "who hastened to prepare it," you cannot slaughter a calf and cook it in a few minutes. Real hospitality takes time. Perhaps in an ancient context, preparing bread from flour and butchering a cow to serve to your guests is the equivalent of a tray of crackers and cold cuts, yet I think we are intended to slow the narrative down and reflect on such involved preparation. Hospitality inherently calls for attention to one's guests and offering them the best that one has to give. That cannot be rushed.

The ancient world in general revered hospitality; and the Israelites, because of their own sojourn in a foreign land and wandering in the desert, were called upon to show compassion and hospitality to strangers and to protect them from harm (Exod 23:9; Lev 19:33-34). Abraham's hospitality, perhaps even beyond the call of ancient hospitality, leads to a blessing from the three men. The text presents these three as mysteriously related to God, whose will they seem to represent, but we also see in Abraham's behavior the precursor to Jesus' parable of the Sheep and the Goats in Matthew 25. In this parable Jesus says that when caring for those in need— the hungry, the thirsty, the stranger—one is caring for Jesus himself.

Ultimately, Jesus links hospitality in this parable to the greatest blessing, that of eternal life.

The focus on hospitality never wavered among the Jewish people and continued with the rise of the church. Jesus receives hospitality from two of his friends, Martha and Mary; but as with many of Jesus' encounters, his response to the hospitality his friends give him challenges us to expand our horizons.

Martha is the more active sister, inviting Jesus in and caring for his physical needs, but she "was distracted by her many tasks" and confronted Jesus, asking, "Lord, do you not care that my sister has left me to do all the work by myself? Tell her then to help me."

Jesus acknowledges the goodness in Martha's hospitality, but points to her sister Mary as the model of hospitality: "There is need of only one thing. Mary has chosen the better part, which will not be taken away from her."

What is that better part? It is attention to the needs of the guest, the Lord himself, as Martha has identified Jesus, and that attention can take the form of physical hospitality. But more important, it is attention to whatever one's guest needs. In this case, attention to Jesus, and not one's own sense of being slighted by a sister who does not do her fair share of the work, is what truly matters. It is what Abraham offered by pouring out on his guests his undivided attention. Hebrews 13:2 says that by doing this, he "entertained angels without knowing it." Yet here Martha has Jesus with her, and she is more concerned with her needs. If she would focus on Jesus, she would have all that she needs.

It is this subtle final insight, which Jesus offers to Martha, that is at the heart of an apparently unrelated passage in Colossians in which Paul rejoices "in my sufferings for your sake." In this passage, Paul says he is "completing what is lacking in Christ's afflictions for the sake of his body, that is, the church." The greatest hospitality Paul can offer, which any of us can offer, is to invite all to participate in the welcoming of Jesus as his servants, in order "to make the word of God fully known, the mystery that has been hidden throughout the ages and generations but has now been revealed to his saints." We do so, as Mary did, by focusing on the "better part," Jesus himself, but serving the stranger, like Abraham, knowing that with the stranger is God.

Imagine yourself sitting at the feet of Jesus, listening to him. Does anything distract you from offering him your full attention and service?

THe Innocent

Seventeenth Sunday in Ordinary Time

Readings: Gen 18:20-32; Ps 138:1-8;
Col 2:12-14; Luke 11:1-13

"On the day I called, you answered me." (Ps 138:3)

In every age, evil takes on a new name and a new face: Auschwitz, sexual abuse, Sodom, human trafficking. The personification of God in the Old Testament takes many forms, but goodness remains the same and unchanged: God who loves us and desires relationship with us. In Genesis 18, God is presented as examining the situation in Sodom and Gomorrah, saying: "How great is the outcry against Sodom and Gomorrah and how very grave their sin! I must go down and see whether they have done altogether according to the outcry that has come to me; and if not, I will know." According to the portrayal of God in Genesis, God does not prejudge the situation but comes to examine it personally.

The presentation of God as actively involved in many scenes in the Old Testament is not ultimately intended to create a notion of an anthropomorphic God, who literally walks among us, but to heighten the notion of the "personal God" who cares for creation and communicates the divine will to men and women. Yet in the same way, it indicates that human beings are intended to be in conversation with God, to make known the needs and desires of the human heart. As such, God does not simply make known a desire to crush the people of Sodom and Gomorrah, nor does Abraham simply turn meekly away from God, but a conversation is presented to us.

God and Abraham deliberate on the fate of the cities of Sodom and Gomorrah, with Abraham negotiating on behalf of the soon to be destroyed cities, campaigning on behalf of the people of these cities. Abraham gently pleads his case, arguing downward the number of righteous people required to secure a reprieve for the notorious cities. Abraham asks that if only a few righteous people could be found, say ten: "Far be it from you to do such a thing, to make the innocent die with the guilty so that the innocent and the guilty would be treated alike! Should not the judge of all the world act with justice?"

As Genesis presents the interaction, God is prepared to be swayed and is persuaded by the intercessions of Abraham, accepting his pleas on behalf of the hoped-for righteous in Sodom and Gomorrah. The evocative scene points to the truth of the claim made by the great Jewish medieval philosopher Moses Maimonides, that God will never turn from a promise of mercy, but will rescind a promise of punishment. It points, that is, to the (inter-)personal nature of God, the justness of God, and the desire to turn from justice and offer mercy, if only the guilty turn away from sin and toward God.

Not only is God open to the intercessions of Abraham, we learn from Jesus in Luke 11 that God desires all of our intercessions, and even more our perseverance in prayer. God does not desire the death of any person— whether guilty or innocent—but wants us to turn our desires to God's kingdom and orient our wills to God's. We pray for the coming of the kingdom, for the perseverance to seek God at all times, night and day, and for the wisdom to know that "if you then, who are evil, know how to give good gifts to your children, how much more will the heavenly Father give the Holy Spirit to those who ask him!" God desires that we, like Abraham, intercede with God, for this indicates our desire to claim our relationship with God and deepen it according to the contours of God's ways and being.

At the heart of God's way and being is the hope that we all find ourselves among the innocent, that we reject the false splendor of the guilty, a way of life suffused with sin, for it is sin that is finally all that needs to be destroyed. If it was us God wanted to destroy, it could have been done long ago, in any way, for numerous reasons, but God desires us in relationship and life. It is for this reason that Colossians tells us that "even when you were dead in transgressions and the uncircumcision of your flesh, he brought you to life along with him, having forgiven us all our transgressions; obliterating the bond against us, with its legal claims, which was opposed to us, he also removed it from our midst, nailing it to the cross." Let the guilt go; God wants us to be the innocent.

Reflect on Abraham's discussions with God. Do you bring all of your requests, pleas, and appeals to God?

THE Inheritance

Eighteenth Sunday in Ordinary Time

Readings: Eccl 1:2; 2:21-23; Ps 90:3-17;
Col 3:1-11; Luke 12:13-21

*"One's life does not consist in the abundance
of possessions."* (Luke 12:15)

The preacher, Qoheleth, says that "all things are vanity!" His intent is not, I think, to be cynical, though Qoheleth can provoke this among the world-weary. His wisdom is rather the product of a hard-boiled realism, which knows the truth of desires and ambitions that often consume us. He speaks of the shortness of life and the ambitions that have driven us, only to have found them unsatisfying. "Here is one who has labored with wisdom and knowledge and skill, and yet to another who has not labored over it, he must leave property. This also is vanity and a great misfortune." Does this reality bother you? Make you sad? "This also is vanity."

Here is the wisdom of this ancient Sam Spade in a nutshell: The things you thought would make you happy probably will not. And if they do make you happy, it will be for only a short while because soon you will die. What seem like the musings of a melancholic scribe, however, are transformed into a bracing wake-up call for those with their eye on the living God. Vanity is vanity, but those who act with God in mind and heart know that their desires and ambitions can be transformed from that which consumes them to that which awakens them to truth.

In the Gospel of Luke, someone makes a request of Jesus that on the surface seems like a reasonable request to make of a teacher known for his wisdom: "Teacher, tell my brother to divide the family inheritance with me." Jesus' reply evinces more of Qoheleth than might initially be apparent, as he gets behind what appears to be an innocent request for equality to a simmering desire for things that indicate a life in tune with vanity, not with God. Jesus warns the petitioner, and through him all of us, to "be on your guard against all kinds of greed; for one's life does not consist in the abundance of possessions." The bluntness of Jesus' response is still bracing—a statement we ought to repeat quietly to ourselves any-time we become convinced we need more money and possessions.

Jesus then tells a parable, his way of speaking across time to every class, gender, and generation, about a rich man. The rich man had land that "produced abundantly." In thinking rationally about the situation, the rich man decided to expand his operations, so he determined to "pull down my barns and build larger ones, and there I will store all my grain and my goods." It is hard to see much wrong with this plan of action. His crops were successful; he needed bigger barns, so he planned to build bigger barns. The parable, found only in Luke, gives us a significant clue, though, as to why this rich man's plans are evidence of vanity and not just good planning.

Considering his plans for new barns to house his abundant crop, the rich man said, "I will say to my soul, Soul, you have ample goods laid up for many years; relax, eat, drink, be merry." One word here opens us up to his foolish vanity and to a vanity so many of us do battle with regularly: soul (*psychê*). He was not vain because he had many physical goods and would have his earthly needs cared for—God knows we need these things—but because he equated his financial success and security with the well-being of his soul. The fool saw his goods as his alone, not as the product of God's bounty intended for him but also for all who are in need. In the parable he twice addresses his soul's health and mistakes his suc-cess on earth for his eternal well-being. It is because of this basic confusion that God in the parable said to him: "You fool! This very night your life is being demanded of you. And the things you have prepared, whose will they be?" We could easily add to the parable a closing epitaph: "This also is vanity."

This life offers numerous paths, and we all must travel one with greater or less success according to the standards of this world. It is not the fact that we must travel a path that creates a fog of vanity, but that we see our earthly rewards as the measure of our life, storing up physical treasures and thinking they purify our souls, while God is asking us to be rich to those in need and rich in the ways of God.

As you stand in the crowd, listening to Jesus' parable, what sorts of vanity do you most need to be on guard against?

An Alert Faith

Nineteenth Sunday in Ordinary Time

Readings: Wis 18:6-9; Ps 33:1-22;
Heb 11:1-19; Luke 12:32-48

"For where your treasure is, there also will your heart be."
(Luke 12:34)

People of faith find themselves often, perhaps daily, tottering on the precipice of disillusion, swaying from their own questions, wondering if they have been suckered by some mug's game that tells them to be satisfied with God's promises instead of the cold, hard reality of this world's guarantees. Still, the claims of faith are not so easy to shake, not in spite of the cold, hard reality of this world's guarantees but because the guarantees of this world are so cold and hard. Sober reflection allows us to see that faith, supposedly ephemeral, vague, and airy, grounds itself on the rock of history, masterfully building on the hope and love of those who have come before us, who have heard, recorded and lived God's word.

Yet even among the earliest Christians, faith could waver, replaced by the concerns and worries of the day. The time of Jesus' Parousia, or "return," which all his earliest disciples hoped was imminent, would work itself out, as it still is working itself out in history. In Luke's gospel, Jesus tells his disciples to "sell your possessions, and give alms. Make purses for yourselves that do not wear out, an unfailing treasure in heaven, where no thief comes near and no moth destroys. For where your treasure is, there your heart will be also." The strong contrast between earthly wealth and heavenly treasure was essential, for the heavenly vision demanded faith; and in the interim between Jesus' ascension and his return, weariness in the contemplation of unseen promises could drag down faith. Jesus pleaded that we be diligent in seeing where the true treasure is.

Alertness is essential for maintaining faith in the true treasure. Drowsy disciples, then and now, need to be awakened, "for the Son of Man is coming at an unexpected hour." The prophecy of Jesus' return claims us, for it is a divinely given word that remains in effect throughout history until it comes to fruition at the end of history.

It is not as if this task were given to us alone. All who came before us needed to maintain the same faithfulness and alertness. The author of the letter to the Hebrews says about the cloud of witnesses who had come even before the apostolic age, "All of these died in faith without having received the promises, but from a distance they saw and greeted them. They confessed that they were strangers and foreigners on the earth, for people who speak in this way make it clear that they are seeking a homeland. If they had been thinking of the land that they had left behind, they would have had opportunity to return." This is the key for the faithful witnesses of old, that the promises of an unseen home were accepted in faith and maintained throughout their lives in the hope of faith.

Their earthly vision had been adjusted so that they could see the truth through the ephemera of hard facts. The author of Hebrews proclaims that "they desire a better country, that is, a heavenly one." These promises have found faithful witnesses not only in the ancient past but throughout history. Faith is not a dead letter, but a lived experience.

Years ago, when I was a teenager, my great-aunt Sarah, then in her nineties, hugged me for what would be the last time and whispered something in my ear that made me cry. She was born in Russia and lost her fiancé in the chaos of the Russian Revolution. She never married and lived on a small farm with two of her unmarried sisters, victims themselves of the travails of the revolution and emigration to a foreign land, whose language they never spoke. This is what made the tears I cried so remarkable. I could not understand what my Tante Sarah had said to me in Low German. I turned to my mother and asked, "What did she say?" My Mother explained: "She said, 'If I don't see you here on earth again, I will see you in heaven.'"

That is faith. And as the years go by, whenever heaven or the God who calls us home to dwell there seem like illusions, that faith becomes more solid, more real to me, for "faith is the assurance of things hoped for, the conviction of things not seen."

Think of God's faithfulness to you and how God has been able to assure and comfort you even in the midst of wavering.

THE FLame OF TruTH

Twentieth Sunday in Ordinary Time

Readings: Jer 38:4-10; Ps 40:2-18;
Heb 12:1-4; Luke 12:49-53

"I have come to set the earth on fire." (Luke 12:49)

It can be hard to tell the truth. Sometimes no one wants to hear it, either because people have already determined a path they feel is more advantageous to them or they are more comfortable ignoring it. Sometimes, we are all those people. For those who read Flannery O'Connor, the shocking realization is not the comeuppance that truth grants her self-righteous, self-satisfied characters, but the grace that shines forth from her stories as they illuminate the dark recesses of our own souls, and we realize: I am that man or woman who has run, and perhaps is still running, from the truth.

In one of the stories in O'Connor's collection *A Good Man Is Hard to Find and Other Stories* (New York: Harcourt Brace Jovanovich, 1977), Mr. Head, after denying knowledge of his grandson Nelson to a group of strangers on an Atlanta street, "stood appalled, judging himself with the thoroughness of God, while the action of mercy covered his pride like a flame and consumed it. He had never thought himself a great sinner before, but he saw now that his true depravity had been hidden from him lest it cause him despair. He realized that he was forgiven for sins from the beginning of time, when he had conceived in his own heart the sin of Adam, until the present, when he had denied poor Nelson" (270).

Why did Mr. Head deny his grandson? Why did the Israelite princes throw the prophet Jeremiah into a muddy well? They denied the truth because it embarrassed them or angered them, frustrated their intentions or challenged them to change their own way of thinking. The truth can make you an outcast—quite literally in Jeremiah's case—put you in danger or disrupt your life. But if we are drawn to the truth, if our hearts are restless until they rest in God, why do we fight against the truth and turn from God?

As Mr. Head says, he had never thought himself a great sinner, but the truth revealed what he had hidden and what most of us want to hide from others and ourselves: we are all great sinners. Others take a different tack, not ignoring sin but reveling in it, denying its very reality, as the late Jim Carroll sang: "Nothing is true, everything is permitted." In this vortex of sin, which permeates the cosmos and our beings, the truth was revealed in Jesus, who knew that his incarnation would create a dividing line. "Do you think that I have come to bring peace to the earth? No, I tell you, but rather division!"

In Jesus' outline of the divisions he would create, he speaks of divisions in families, the building block of society then and now, the place where each of us belongs. He sketches a dreadful reality in which "five in one household will be divided, three against two and two against three." In families then and now, divisions grounded in sin break apart the fundamental structure of human relationship.

Jesus' desire was not to create division, but to create acceptance of the truth that he embodies; but as long as there is sin shot through human hearts, the heart most crooked, there will be attempts to turn aside from the truth, to deny the truth, and even to deny that there is truth. But there is a remedy. The author of Hebrews asks us to

> lay aside every weight and the sin that clings so closely, and let us run with perseverance the race that is set before us, looking to Jesus the pioneer and perfecter of our faith, who for the sake of the joy that was set before him endured the cross, disregarding its shame, and has taken his seat at the right hand of the throne of God. Consider him who endured such hostility against himself from sinners, so that you may not grow weary or lose heart.

In considering this reality, Mr. Head had a realization: "He saw that no sin was too monstrous for him to claim as his own, and since God loved in proportion as He forgave, he felt ready at that instant to enter paradise" (270). The truth is that God wants us to lay our burden down and accept the eternal invitation.

Imagine yourself in conversation with Jesus. What truths do you need to share so that you do not grow weary or lose heart?

ALL THE Nations

Twenty-First Sunday in Ordinary Time

Readings: Isa 66:18-21; Ps 117:1-2;
Heb 12:5-17; Luke 13:22-30

"Lord, will only a few be saved?" (Luke 13:23)

The question was put to Jesus, "Lord, will only a few be saved?" His answer, like many a teacher's answer regarding more mundane matters, like quizzes and tests, is a variation on "study hard." Jesus instructs the questioner and the crowd, "Strive to enter through the narrow door; for many, I tell you, will try to enter and will not be able." It is one of those non-answers that teachers and parents will often give, because the answer is indeed dependent upon the response of the student or child. First Timothy 2:4 encapsulates the hope of the whole church when the author writes that God "desires everyone to be saved and to come to the knowledge of the truth," but Jesus' exhortation to "strive" is not necessarily an argument that few will be saved, but an argument against presumption on the part of those who believe they have already checked every multiple-choice item correctly.

According to the prophet Isaiah, the presumptions of the people of Israel, if narrowly conceived, needed to be broadened. The word of God came to the prophet: "I am coming to gather all nations and tongues; and they shall come and shall see my glory." All the nations would hear of God's glory and see God's glory. Through the missions of the first apostles and their successors, clergy and lay, the word of God went to all the nations. It is a shocking reality when put in historical perspective, especially if considered apart from the work of the Holy Spirit in the church. A few Jewish men and women, transformed by the person of Jesus Christ, enveloped by the Holy Spirit, set about to shape Isaiah's prophetic and symbolic language into real events. And they did.

As Jesus continued to teach, he sketched scenarios in which those who presumably knew him—"We ate and drank with you, and you taught in our streets"—were chastened with his blunt reply, "I do not know where you come from; go away from me, all you evildoers!" Why such a response? It is directed at the presumption that "knowing" is sufficient for entrance to the kingdom. It is not a sign that Jesus is longing to keep people out of the kingdom. Jesus rejects instead the assumption that proximity and nearness to the things of God are substitutes for a desperate hunger to live out the word of God. There is no corner of the world in which a person cannot yearn, work for, and be joined to the reign of God.

We hope that all answer the call of the church, that it will be a house stretched beyond walls built with human hands. This is not a hope for a few, but a hope for the whole world redeemed. Still, Jesus warns: "There will be weeping and gnashing of teeth when you see Abraham and Isaac and Jacob and all the prophets in the kingdom of God, and you yourselves thrown out. Then people will come from east and west, from north and south, and will eat in the kingdom of God." The messianic banquet is prepared for all those who choose to respond to God's call, and this will include delegates of the whole of humanity; in the beautiful shorthand of Jesus' teaching, people will come from every direction under the sun. And whole of humanity includes the prophets; and Abraham, Isaac, and Jacob; and the people of Israel, who themselves carried the revelation to the world and who foresaw its universal fulfillment.

The whole human family has been called to be saved, for we are all children of the same Father. In the context of Hebrews 12:5-17, we might even render the word *saved* by the phrase "child of God," for the passage describes how God "disciplines" the children of God in order to conform to God's will. The Greek word that is translated here as "discipline" is *paideia*. It is essential to understand that the word *paideia*, which appears seven times in this passage, means "education," not simply physical discipline. God is educating us for the kingdom. If it is not precisely tests that we must take, the author of Hebrews speaks of us "enduring" *paideia*, or God's education, so that when asked, "Will only a few be saved?" we can confidently answer, "Strive to enter through the narrow door," for God "desires everyone to be saved and to come to the knowledge of the truth."

Reflect on the *paideia*, education or discipline, by which God has instructed you. What has God taught you to prepare for the kingdom?

THE CITY OF THE LIVING GOD

Twenty-Second Sunday in Ordinary Time

Readings: Sir 3:17-29; Ps 68:4-11;
Heb 12:18-24; Luke 14:1-14

*"When you hold a banquet, invite the poor, the crippled,
the lame, the blind."* (Luke 14:13)

Most readers of this column have been in a position of authority at some time, I'm sure; and some of us, this writer included, enjoy a constancy of authority because of education, ordination, position, or wealth. Though we might not speak of it often, even quietly to ourselves, it is a delight to have honor and prestige. This delight is not denied by Jesus, but in a parable found in today's readings he turns honorable prestige on its head.

To understand the parable, we must understand the function of honor and shame, not just in ancient Palestine, but in our own lives today. It is true that honor and shame function differently in our day than in Jesus' day, but there is something profoundly human about our need for the one and our aversion to the other.

Jesus uses two examples from a banquet to illustrate our desire for honor and our loathing of shame, yet even as he does this, he recalibrates the meaning of both. In the first example, he instructs his hearers not to seek seats of honor at a banquet, since they might be shamed if someone with greater honor appears and demands his rightful due. In the second example, Jesus encourages his audience to seek out the weak, the poor, and the lame for their banquet, not their friends and relatives, since to invite those nearest and dearest just leads to reciprocation, a repayment of hospitality in the here and now. The recalibration comes in learning the true source of honor and shame and the true means of repayment.

The first example Jesus offers does not deny the desire for honor or the longing to avoid embarrassment, but he suggests that humility is the best path for both outcomes. Instead of reclining "at table in the place of honor" at a banquet and then being humbled when "a more distinguished guest" arrives, Jesus instructs that "when you are invited, go and take the lowest place so that when the host comes to you he may say, 'My friend, move up to a higher position.' Then you will enjoy the esteem of your companions at the table."

Ben Sira echoes this point: "My child, perform your tasks with humility; then you will be loved by those whom God accepts." People do appreciate humility—not abject self-negation or self-hatred—because it does not place itself at or as the center of attention, seeking to have all needs met by others or ignoring the claims of others.

This remains suitable advice for those embarrassing dinner party moments even today—just consult Miss Manners—but Jesus' point lies deeper. He says that "everyone who exalts himself will be humbled, but the one who humbles himself will be exalted." Humility will save you from embarrassment today and might even lead to a higher position at the banquet, but the exaltation Jesus is speaking of has to do with the messianic banquet at the end of time—that is, places at table in the city of the living God.

Why this is the case can be seen in the second example Jesus gives. Jesus offers the strange advice—imagine Thanksgiving or Christmas—not to invite "your friends or your brothers or your relatives or your wealthy neighbors, in case they may invite you back and you have repayment." But "when you hold a banquet, invite the poor, the crippled, the lame, the blind; blessed indeed will you be because of their inability to repay you. For you will be repaid at the resurrection of the righteous." Jesus instructs us to expand our notion of God's family to include those most in need of food, those most in need of honor since shame has been forced upon them.

True honor is found in humility, and true humility is located in seeking the needs of others, not one's own. Honor might never be gained in this world for seeking out the poor and the needy, and repayment might come only in the new age, when honor and shame, like poverty and wealth, are burned up in the glory of God. At the banquet in the city of God, all sit in positions of equal rank and all share in the grace that reveals us all to be members of God's one family.

Reflect on a banquet to which all have been invited, including the poor, the crippled, the lame, and the blind. Do you see yourself as a part of the family or set apart from the crowd?

DO THE RIGHT THING

Twenty-Third Sunday in Ordinary Time

Readings: Wis 9:13-18; Ps 90:3-17;
Phlm 9-17; Luke 14:25-33

"Welcome him as you would me." (Phlm 17)

The common understanding of the relationship between Onesimus and Philemon in Paul's letter to Philemon is that Onesimus was a slave of Philemon. Though it remains a debated issue, Onesimus had either run away from Philemon or had been sent by him to render service to Paul while he was imprisoned. During this time, Onesimus had become Paul's "child" and Paul his "father," Pauline language that indicates the conversion of Onesimus to the Christian faith. Paul and Onesimus were now part of the same family.

This spiritual conversion also indicated for Paul a necessary change in the relationship between Onesimus and Philemon. Philemon was to receive Onesimus back "no longer as a slave but more than a slave, a brother, beloved especially to me, but even more so to you, as a man and in the Lord." Paul offers this loaded assessment of the necessity of Philemon's compliance: "So if you regard me as a partner, welcome him as you would me." Onesimus might have left home as a slave, a "living tool," in the language of Aristotle, but he was coming home as a beloved son and brother, "as a man."

The story of Onesimus is a challenge when we consider the ancient reality of slavery and the fact that Christians in the first centuries of the Common Era owned slaves, but the continuing challenge is that we allow our Christian faith to work on social evils that enslave people still today. Our conversions of heart must allow us to see people as potential brothers and sisters and not things to be used for our benefit. While slavery does not exist today de jure, there are many forms of de facto slavery, and experts in modern slavery and human trafficking suggest that there are more slaves today than ever before in history.

Paul's treatment of Onesimus offers us a model for treating every person as a potential child, sister, or brother. In a short time, Onesimus had become, in Paul's words, "my own heart." A number of commentators have wondered why Paul would not simply demand that Philemon release Onesimus from slavery instead of await his "consent, so that the good you do might not be forced but voluntary"; but because slavery was legal in the Roman Empire, Paul had little legal standing to make demands. What he did have, however, was standing as a moral guide and teacher, and he called on his "brother" to do the right thing. He called on Philemon, that is, to be converted and to welcome back a brother and not a slave.

We, however, do not face the conundrum of the legality of slavery or human trafficking as Paul did; they are illegal practices. Yet slavery flourishes underground, hidden away or hidden in plain sight. Our response is, therefore, clear and obvious: we must not engage in activities that allow the dehumanization of our brothers and sisters to continue, whether that is participating in pornography, the sex trade, or other forms of exploitation of human beings. Our task is to work toward the conversion of both exploiter and exploited, just as Paul did, so that both human and spiritual freedom can be enjoyed by all. When we say no to sin, the cement of injustice starts to crumble.

It is in this context that the shocking, even bewildering, teaching of Jesus on the nature of discipleship might be unraveled. Jesus says, "If anyone comes to me without hating his father and mother, wife and children, brothers and sisters, and even his own life, he cannot be my disciple." Hate is a strong word, best understood to mean, "You cannot love anything more than me." But this linguistic adjustment does not dilute the theological teaching. Calculate the cost of discipleship and measure it against all that you hold dear. Are you willing to turn away from the comforts of social propriety to follow Jesus? Are you willing to challenge the unjust structures of sin? Are you all in? Just as Jesus suggests for his disciples, Paul was all in. He was able to challenge his brother in the Lord to see in a slave the face of God and the face of family. In the enigmatic teaching of the gospel, when you begin to "hate" your family, the true extent of family is revealed and your brothers and sisters multiplied beyond counting.

Imagine yourself listening to Jesus' teaching about family. What do you need to let go, so your understanding of family can grow?

WHO'S MISSING?

Twenty-Fourth Sunday in Ordinary Time

Readings: Exod 32:7-14; Ps 51:3-19;
1 Tim 1:12-17; Luke 15:1-32

"I will rise and go to my father." (Luke 15:18)

When you're lost, it's good to be missed; it's even better to be found. At the heart of spiritual lostness, though, is our collusion in our own absence. People are not inanimate objects like coins, things that can fall unwittingly into corners, nor are they like sheep, animals with limited understanding of the repercussions of their wandering ways. When people stray spiritually, they act with free will, although it can be restricted by previous experiences, ignorance, and naïveté. Still, people walk away from God, generally because we are convinced we know better than God does what is best for us.

During the Exodus, God spoke to Moses, saying: "Go down at once to your people, whom you brought out of the land of Egypt, for they have become depraved. They have soon turned aside from the way I pointed out to them, making for themselves a molten calf and worshiping it, sacrificing to it and crying out, 'This is your God, O Israel, who brought you out of the land of Egypt!'"

Should we file this under "How soon they forget" or "What have you done for me lately"? Moses intervenes, imploring God to preserve the people about whom God had said, "I will make your descendants as numerous as the stars in the sky," and the Lord "relented in the punishment he had threatened to inflict on his people."

It is not that God in the Old Testament is hungry to punish the people of Israel, or wrongdoers in general; God is not pulled back from the fight, screaming, "Let me at them," conjuring up some other plan to wreak deadly revenge. The issue is what we deserve. The biblical accent can fall on what we have earned through our own stubborn behavior and God's merciful relenting, as in Exodus, or it can fall on God's merciful search for those who are lost because of their own stubborn behavior. Wherever the accent falls, the word is always mercy and the necessity is repentance, the turn back to God.

Jesus tells a story of two lost sons, the younger one, who has wandered far from home and "squandered his inheritance," and the older one, who has stayed near his father on his estate. The youngest son winds up wasting his inheritance and living with pigs, eating the husks of pig food. At some point the wandering son realizes it is time to go home and beg for mercy from his father. He has not lost only his money; he has lost himself. The father spies him from a long way off, runs to his son, embraces him and kisses him.

But it was when the younger son recognized that he was lost, that he had made choices that reduced him to physical and spiritual poverty, that he could repent and be found. It was only then that he could come home to be showered not with reproach but with mercy.

The older son is another matter. He has remained near to his father, but it seems he is not close to him. He resents his younger brother coming home to a feast and his father for throwing the feast. He is angry that mercy has been shown, and when his father comes to plead with him to celebrate, he spews out the grievances he has been nursing for many years: "Look, all these years I served you and not once did I disobey your orders."

The older brother cannot celebrate his sibling's return because he has no joy in the father's presence. Life with his father has been a burden, an unwelcome task, a plodding life in which he has struggled not to "disobey your orders." Can the older son see that he is lost? You can only be found when you know you are lost and it is time to come home.

Many of us fall into the category of the older son, but it does not matter where we are as long as we make it home, for either "you are here with me always; everything I have is yours" or "we must celebrate and rejoice, because your brother was dead and has come to life again; he was lost and has been found." Regardless of which category we fall into, an invitation has been issued: Party at God's house. Everyone's invited.

Place yourself in the parable of the Two Sons. Which son (or daughter) are you and what do you need to grasp or let go in order to celebrate?

Commending DISHONESTY

Twenty-Fifth Sunday in Ordinary Time

Readings: Amos 8:4-7; Ps 113:1-8;
1 Tim 2:1-8; Luke 16:1-13

"How much do you owe my master?" (Luke 16:5)

I am not alone in considering Jesus' parable of the Dishonest (or un-righteous, *adikia*) Manager (or steward, *oikonomos*) the most difficult, complex, and confusing of all Jesus' parables. The reason for this is simple: in the first verse of the parable, after determining that the manager is "squandering his property," the rich man relieves him of his position; but after the manager subsequently and unilaterally reduces the payments owed to the rich man by his debtors, the rich man praises his fired manager "for acting prudently."

How are we to balance his loss of position with the commendation? And what exactly did he do to deserve commendation? Does the manager get a reference letter even after being fired for slashing the liability of his master's debtors?

The tensions in this parable work because we struggle to understand how everyone fits in this scenario. Does the rich man represent God? Who are the debtors? Do they represent everyone in relationship to God? Or are these specifically followers of Jesus? But who is the manager? If the rich man represents God, does the manager stand for the leadership of the church?

More important than wondering what or who every character in the parable represents, however, is the question of how to understand the whole notion of debt. In this parable the debt is measured by jugs of olive oil and bushels of wheat; but often when Jesus talks about debt, he is referring to spiritual debt. On the other hand, throughout Luke's gospel, how people use their possessions and resources has implications and repercussions for their spiritual health.

It is true that the final verses offer explanations of the parable, but while these verses offer valuable insight into the contrast between money and true spiritual wealth and the need to be honest in all dealings, large and small, they do not answer the central problem of the parable: Why is the dishonest manager commended?

It is important first of all to understand the role of the ancient steward, who managed whole estates for absentee landlords, including the tenant farmers, but was often a slave born on the estate, as explained by the Roman agricultural writer Columella (first century AD). The *oikonomos* had a degree of freedom in how he ran the estate, but he was ultimately answerable to the owner. Earlier in Luke (12:40–42), Peter asked Jesus to explain a parable about the return of the Son of Man and whether the parable was "for us," the apostles, "or for everyone." Jesus replied, "Who then is the faithful and prudent manager [*oikonomos*] whom his master will put in charge of his slaves, to give them their allowance of food at the proper time?" It seems likely, then, that the manager in this parable stands for leaders who represent Jesus in his absence.

The "squandering of property" (the same verb is used in Luke 15:13 to describe the younger son's wastefulness in the parable of the Two Sons) for which the manager is dismissed has not to do so much with actual olive oil or wheat, but with the mistreatment of the tenants of the estate by the manager, who have had their debt enlarged to meet his needs, not those of the rich man. This is why the reduction of the tenants' debts, the lessening of their burden, leads ultimately to commendation for the manager, even as he loses his position.

Of true value to the rich man, God, is not wheat or olive oil, but the care of his tenants laboring in his fields. When the manager reduces the debt of the farmers, he finally understands the nature of true wealth and the nature of his master, the rich man. Yes, the *oikonomos* wanted to improve his own position, but in so doing he genuinely released debt. The debtors have debt forgiven, and the relationship between the owner of the estate and his tenant farmers is improved. Forgiveness has eternal value.

The lesson of the lessening, after all, is not for the characters in the parable, but for us. If it is valuable for us as leaders or members of the church to forgive the debts of others as a last-minute gambit to save our skin, how much more valuable is it not to pile up debt against others to begin with but to forgive radically from the start? How much do you owe me? How much do you owe my master? I can't even remember. I'm not even keeping track.

Imagine yourself sitting alongside Jesus as he tells the parable of the Dishonest Manager. What debts do you need to forgive?

RICH Man, POOr Man

Readings: Amos 6:1-7; Ps 146:7-10;
1 Tim 6:11-16; Luke 16:19-31

"The rich man also died and was buried." (Luke 16:22)

Paul's first letter to Timothy, though many scholars doubt Paul wrote it, reflects the heart of the Christian hope that Paul expressed in his letters: "Fight the good fight of the faith; take hold of the eternal life, to which you were called and for which you made the good confession in the presence of many witnesses." At the end of this letter, Timothy is encouraged to imitate "Christ Jesus, who in his testimony before Pontius Pilate made the good confession" and "to keep the commandment without spot or blame until the manifestation of our Lord Jesus Christ." It is at the coming of Christ Jesus that the fullness of him "who is the blessed and only Sovereign, the King of kings and Lord of lords" will be displayed. This is the cosmic perspective that makes kings, tyrants, presidents, celebrities, nobles, and rich men and women seem small or, rather, allows them to be viewed in the proper light: they are people like everyone else, not inherently better, not inherently worse, created by God for the "unapproachable light" of divinity, not for the passing glory, honor, and riches of this world.

But it is hard to be humble, or to share, when you are the rich man and your perspective is narrowed to this world or, even narrower, to one's own desires. Jesus tells what seems like a simple parable in Luke 16 about a rich man and a poor man. But the poor man has a name, which alerts us that this parable may not be as simple as it seems. After all, whose name do you know better, Bill Gates or the beggar on the downtown street corner? But here we learn that the poor man's name is Lazarus, while the rich man's name remains unknown. Yet no one is nameless to God. We are all known by name, whether rich or poor; and no one, in the eyes of God, is superior to another. Our worth, our inherent belovedness, is not based on who we are but what we are: human beings created in the image of God.

There is another point about Lazarus' name that is even more telling for this specific parable. The rich man seems to be separated from Lazarus and God only because of his wealth, which seems unjust, improper, simply not fitting. Why should earthly wealth condemn one to an eternal life of misery? The parable is subtle, however; the clue to why the rich man is judged is in the details. Lazarus lay in misery by the rich man's gate for a long time, begging for food, but his pleas were not heard. Rather, they were ignored. How do we know this? In the parable it is the rich man who identifies Lazarus by name, when he calls out: "Father Abraham, have pity on me. Send Lazarus to dip the tip of his finger in water and cool my tongue, for I am suffering torment in these flames." If he knows Lazarus by name in the afterworld, he knew Lazarus by name when he begged for mercy and food in this world. But the rich man decided he had better things to do than help the poor man at his gate. That decision to ignore the poor, Jesus demonstrates for us, has eternal implications.

Even accounting for the rich man's turning away from Lazarus, the issue of wealth still discomfits. It does seem that there is something inherently distracting about worldly riches that focus our attention on earthly pleasures. In the parable Abraham says, "Child, remember that during your lifetime you received your good things, and Lazarus in like manner evil things; but now he is comforted here, and you are in agony." This is properly frightening, for it does suggest a kind of quid pro quo, where the "good things" of this life equate to agony in the life to come and "evil things" in this life to comfort in the world to come. Is this a necessary outcome?

No, for Jesus, throughout Luke and all of the gospels, suggests that proper use of wealth can have positive implications both for those in need now and for the life to come. It is especially pertinent for those of us who are wealthier than we want to admit. We need to be certain about what truly matters to us, for it matters now and it matters eternally.

Reflect on Lazarus sitting at your gate. When you see him, how do you want to befriend him?

A LITTLe FaITH

Twenty-Seventh Sunday in Ordinary Time

Readings: Hab 1:2-3; 2:2-4; Ps 95:1-9;
2 Tim 1:6-14; Luke 17:5-10

"The apostles said to the Lord, 'Increase our faith!'" (Luke 17:5)

"The apostles said to the Lord, 'Increase our faith!'" What's the equation for increasing faith? "The Lord replied, 'If you had faith the size of a mustard seed, you could say to this mulberry tree, "Be uprooted and planted in the sea," and it would obey you.'" What sort of answer is this?

Jesus uses this image of the tiny mustard seed to allow us to conceive both of his kingdom and the faith required by his followers. I have always thought it a sign that we need "more" faith but only have a "little" faith, so little that we cannot produce the faith necessary for great things. The Rev. Tomas Halik, a Czech priest and intellectual, undercuts this understanding in *Night of the Confessor*:

> Suddenly this text spoke to me in a way that differed from the usual interpretation. Isn't Jesus saying to us with these words: Why are you asking me for lots of faith? Maybe your faith is "far too big"? Only if it decreases, until it is as small as a mustard seed, will it give forth its fruit and display its strength. ([New York: Random House, 2012], 17)

Faith, says Halik, might need to be little, to be unencumbered by that which seems solid, necessary, and essential but is brittle, sharp, and rigid, protecting our human endeavors and not our divine faith. Halik sees, at least in the West, easy certainties about religion and ideology that have replaced willingness to suffer for one's faith, a replacement of mystery with easy answers. "Big faith" offers no help against the paradoxes and complexities of life; it seeks safety in numbers and certainty from the past.

But what about what Halik calls the "impossibly absurd" promise that if we had a "little faith" we could move a mulberry tree to the sea? Halik does not believe Jesus is encouraging us to ask for and expect the equivalent of spiritual "superpowers," which might simply play into our "covert narcissism, megalomania, Messiah complex" (25) or that Jesus is encouraging a form of "autosuggestion," by which we replace faith in Christ with "self-affirmation, self-assertiveness, and the 'extension of one's potential'" (26).

Instead, Halik associates this radical expression of faith with behavior deemed foolish by the world, like "forgiving when I could take vengeance, and even 'loving my neighbor,' and 'turning the other cheek' when I have been done wrong to" (26). This absurd little faith of forgiveness and turning the other cheek is in fact living out a life of love in the midst of a world that desires power and vengeance, and seeks always to protect "what's mine." Are not these little acts of love more absurd in our world than moving a mulberry tree into the sea? Do they not require continual little acts of faith in the face of violence, mockery, rejection, and the loss of the things of this world?

So, how do we increase our faith? What Jesus says in the verses that follow comprise a surprising answer, which fits with Halik's focus on the positive nature of "little" faith. In these enigmatic verses, Jesus speaks of master-slave relations, a key aspect of ancient society that every hearer in antiquity would have understood. The language of human slavery properly sounds harsh to modern ears, but in Jesus' day a slave would do what his master required and would not be unduly rewarded or praised for it. Jesus' focus, though, is on the spiritual implications for his followers: "So you also, when you have done all that you were ordered to do, say, 'We are worthless slaves; we have done only what we ought to have done.'"

This is not precisely the language of "self-affirmation, self-assertiveness, and the 'extension of one's potential.'" Faith, Jesus says, is the practice of doing what we ought to do as his followers, however bizarre and absurd it might seem to a world that demands more. It is the image of Paul in prison, "a prisoner for his sake," bearing his "share of hardship for the Gospel with the strength that comes from God." It is the prophet Habakkuk, crying out regarding the "destruction and violence" that surround him and hearing God's voice say, "The vision still has its time, presses on to fulfillment, and will not disappoint; if it delays, wait for it, it will surely come, it will not be late." How do you increase your faith? Practice letting it grow small.

Think of Jesus' faith as the size of a mustard seed. What must you do to let your faith become "small"?

Becoming Clean

Twenty-Eighth Sunday in Ordinary Time

Readings: 2 Kgs 5:14-17; Ps 98:1-4;
2 Tim 2:8-13; Luke 17:11-19

"Jesus, Master, have mercy on us!" (Luke 17:13)

As a child, I saw the world in peculiar ways, as children tend to do, influenced partly by the two powerful forces of television and the Bible. Growing up in the 1960s, I was fairly certain from the movies and TV shows I watched that a good portion of humanity died in quicksand, so I was on guard for quicksand. I was also sure that about half the people who lived at the time of Jesus or Elisha had leprosy. I made no distinction between the Old Testament and New Testament; as far as I knew, Moses, Elisha, and Jesus all lived on the same street. Biblical stories that featured someone afflicted with leprosy jumped out at me. I knew very little about leprosy, but I did know it was devastating and that I would be an outcast if I caught it.

Leprosy in the form that I imagined it, known today as Hansen's disease, did indeed exist at the time of Elisha and Jesus, though biblical "leprosy" denotes many other, milder forms of skin disorder as well. The US Department of Health and Human Services website states that "Hansen's disease, also known as leprosy, is a chronic bacterial disease that primarily affects the skin" and today is "very treatable, and, with early diagnosis and treatment, is not disabling." Still, apart from the physical pain these skin conditions brought, there were the deeper pains that led to psychic, communal, and spiritual disorder. Indeed, even today "Hansen's disease (leprosy) remains the most misunderstood human infectious disease. The stigma long associated with the disease still exists in most of the world, and the psychological and social effects may be more difficult to deal with than the actual physical illness."

Leviticus 13 outlines the religious duties of the priest and of the afflicted person. If the priest found that the person was "unclean," the resulting stigma specified that "the person with such an infectious disease must wear torn clothes, let his hair be unkempt, cover the lower part of his face and cry out, 'Unclean! Unclean!' As long as he has the infection he remains unclean. He must live alone; he must live outside the camp" (Lev 13:45-46). To be unclean in ancient Israel was not to be declared sinful, but to be "out of order" and therefore unable to live in community with the people of God or to worship God in the temple. To distinguish between clean and unclean was God's command and a means by which Israel was to become holy like God (Lev 11:44-47).

The wholeness that we yearn for, physically, spiritually, and emotionally, is at the center of the holiness to which we have been called. The story of Naaman, the Syrian general whom Elisha guides in his restoration to physical wholeness from leprosy, is the story of a Gentile who is "out of order" physically and excluded from God's people. His wholeness is indicated physically when "his flesh was restored like the flesh of a young boy," but his spiritual restoration is manifested when this Gentile warrior's heart turns to the living God. His response is gratitude to Elisha and to the God of Israel, whom Naaman says he will serve from now on, even in a foreign land.

This gratitude for God's mercy and healing is also central to Luke's account of Jesus healing ten lepers. In the liminal region between Samaria and Galilee, the ten cry out to Jesus for mercy. Jesus, following Leviticus 11, directs them to the priests—even though they are not all Jewish—and as they follow his directions they are all healed of their skin disorder. Only one of them, however, returns to Jesus to show his gratitude, and he was a Samaritan, someone "out of order." Jesus asked, "Was none of them found to return and give praise to God except this foreigner?"

Both of these stories indicate, though, that as the person with leprosy is now restored to wholeness, so, too, is the foreigner now welcome home. In recognition of God's action in their lives, gratitude fills them. They are no longer lepers. But even more than this, there need be no more "lepers" of any kind any longer, for no longer must anyone fear separation from God. God has come to welcome you home, to restore true order, to make you clean.

Reflect on a time when you have felt excluded from the church or God. How did you come to feel included again? How can you include others?

An Annoying Faith

Twenty-Ninth Sunday in Ordinary Time

Readings: Exod 17:8-13; Ps 121:1-8;
2 Tim 3:14–4:2; Luke 18:1-8

*"Yet because this widow keeps bothering me,
I will grant her justice."* (Luke 18:5)

"Hey, want to hear the most annoying sound in the world?" That is Jim Carrey's character, Lloyd, speaking in the 1994 comedy *Dumb and Dumber*. He goes on to demonstrate the world's most annoying sound. Some people might find a lowbrow comedy like this, as a whole, a collection of some of the most annoying sounds in the world. Hold on to that thought; this might work out for you spiritually.

It seems that the annoyance factor works two ways. On the one hand, God hears our persistent, bothersome pleas; on the other hand, God asks us to engage in behavior that punctures polite convention. Jesus' parable in Luke regarding the dishonest judge and the annoying widow is one of those biblical passages that takes one aback each time it is encountered. I keep wondering, when I hear of the widow who because of her persistent badgering receives justice from "a judge who neither feared God nor had respect for people," whether I am truly getting the point or missing some profound spiritual insight that my surface reading cannot perceive.

In the parable, Jesus indicates that persistence in bringing our pleas to God in prayer matters. Even the unjust judge grants the wishes of the woman when she will not cease calling out to him, though it must be said he has his own needs in mind. As he explains, he is concerned she will "wear me out by continually coming." But that is the point: if an unjust judge will render a proper verdict when one is persistent in pleading one's case, how much more will God render the proper verdict?

The question I just asked is a way of arguing common among the rabbis, known in Hebrew as a *qal wa-homer* argument, "an implicit argument from the lesser to the greater, and vice-versa." The parable of the annoying

Widow and the Unjust Judge has at its heart an implicit *qal wa-homer* argument.

God is not unjust; God is not unwilling to hear us; God does not render justice just to get rid of us. So if we approach God with our prayers, our pleas, our pain, our suffering, our loneliness, not only will God hear us; God will render justice not to get rid of us and not because we have worn God down with the most annoying sounds in the world, but because God loves us, wants what is best for us, and wants to hear from us, over and over again.

And so, as the parable nears its conclusion, Jesus asks: "Will not God grant justice to his chosen ones who cry to him day and night? Will he delay long in helping them? I tell you, he will quickly grant justice to them."

Yet the parable ends with a question designed to challenge us: "And yet, when the Son of Man comes, will he find faith on earth?"

Do we see God as an unjust judge? Do we see God as unconcerned about our problems? Do we see God as someone who does not want to hear from us? This parable asks us to perceive God properly as the one who desires us, whom we can never annoy, who is more than open to welcoming our concerns. God yearns for us to lay our burdens down.

This is the persistence with which the author of the second letter to Timothy, traditionally identified as Paul, instructs Timothy to live the Christian life. In this passage, Paul functions in the role of a coach as he encourages Timothy to "continue in what you have learned and firmly believed," holding up the Scripture as a faithful guide, for "all Scripture is inspired by God and is useful for teaching, for reproof, for correction, and for training in righteousness."

Paul says that in view of Christ's "appearing and his kingdom," Timothy should "proclaim the message; be persistent whether the time is favorable or unfavorable; convince, rebuke, and encourage, with the utmost patience in teaching."

At stake is our life with God, so we must be persistent in approaching God and in proclaiming the message. The most annoying sound for God, according to Jesus, is our silence, not our persistent knock, knock, knocking on heaven's door. It seems that we are being invited to make some noise, so let's kick up a spiritual racket.

Place yourself at the judge's home in Jesus' parable. What do you need to ask of God, over and over again?

TIrED OF SIN

Thirtieth Sunday in Ordinary Time

Readings: Sir 35:12-18; Ps 34:2-23;
2 Tim 4:6-18; Luke 18:9-14

"O God, be merciful to me a sinner." (Luke 18:13)

Sin is attractive. I have watched a lot of television shows in my life and a lot more commercials, and the one thing I know for certain is that sin is fun, often accompanied by happy young women and men, and there are no, absolutely no, consequences for bad behavior! If you want to be justified in your pathologies, let the pleasure bleed out from the TV screen and wash over you. You will be greeted by an audacity of entitlement for whatever behavior you engage in, secure in the confidence of one who knows that there are no repercussions. This is sin that no longer has the good sense to know what it is.

This experience is not precisely comparable to that of the Pharisee in Jesus' story of the righteous tax collector because the Pharisee in the story still had the good moral sense to recognize the reality of sin and the need to honor God. He prayed: "God, I thank you that I am not like other people: thieves, rogues, adulterers, or even like this tax collector. I fast twice a week; I give a tenth of all my income." There is one parallel, though, and that is his blindness to his own sins. Sin was something others did, and he had tired of their sins; but since he did not acknowledge sin in himself, he remained self-satisfied, happy, and justified.

This ancient scenario also makes clear that it is not fair to blame Madison Avenue for our sins, our sense of entitlement, or our self-righteousness. The attractions of sin, I have it on good authority, are not original to our age. Madison Avenue and the TV networks might commodify our fallen natures and sell them back to us as entertainment, but the vast majority of us conspire with the advertisers and producers in our own downfall. If the media whisper in our ear, they only whisper lies that we delight to repeat to ourselves.

In fact, it is television that has recently put on display for us the effects of sin in as blunt a fashion as possible in the person of Walter White. The main character of the hit TV series *Breaking Bad* continued to tell himself that what he was doing was for the care of his family, even as he left behind a meth empire and numerous dead bodies and lost souls. But Walter White could not manage the damage of sin, and as his twisted empire crumbled, his family ruined or dead, the reality is presented to us starkly: sin is our attempt to meet our own twisted needs, which from the beginning are perversely turned away from God.

Yet Walter White only did on a larger scale what we all do when we turn away from God. He first convinced himself there was no sin and that, even if there were, it was justified. Jesus offers for our consideration a tax collector, crying out to heaven, "God, be merciful to me, a sinner!" Jesus tells us that the tax collector "went down to his home justified rather than the other," the Pharisee. This is the only occurrence of the verb *dikaioô*, "to justify or make righteous," in all of Luke's gospel. It is a perfect participle, which means it might be translated "having been made righteous." Why is this sinner justified? "All who exalt themselves will be humbled, but all who humble themselves will be exalted." To move from self-exaltation to humility to justification, you need to acknowledge your sin and you need to get tired of your sin. You need to get sick of the excuses, the lies, and the entitlement; you need to come home to God.

We tire of sin when we recognize we are intended for more and when we feel God's love burning through the lies we tell ourselves. God does not need a Madison Avenue ad agency presenting his pitch: "Tired of sin? Want to get rid of it? You keep scrubbing and scrubbing but those stubborn, persistent stains won't go? Don't despair, there's a God who cares." All God needs is recognition on the part of the sinner that she is loved. In the presence of God's love, the reality that sin cannot abide becomes gloriously apparent. This is when the cry emerges, "God, be merciful to me, a sinner!" The best part of all? God will be.

Imagine yourself listening to the tax collector cry out to God. What sins do you need to bring to God and let go of?

THE SMALL MATTER OF SIN

Thirty-First Sunday in Ordinary Time

Readings: Wis 11:22–12:2; Ps 145:1-14;
2 Thess 1:11–2:2; Luke 19:1-10

"You overlook people's sins so that they may repent." (Wis 11:23)

The passage from the book of Wisdom about God "overlooking" sins has a wry humor when juxtaposed with little Zacchaeus, too small in stature to be seen. That is not true, of course, for no matter where Zacchaeus was standing, hidden among the crowd or walking away from Jesus, God "sees" our sins. From the story of Adam and Eve, to Cain and Abel, Moses and the Egyptian slave driver, and David and Bathsheba, all of whom try to carry out their acts of disobedience clandestinely, the truth is that sin cannot be hidden from God. Sin needs a solution other than human concealment. Zacchaeus' climbing a tree to see Jesus is simply a sign that he wants to be found by Jesus, that he is seeking the solution.

The solution must be able to coax those who are afraid, scarred, and marred by rejection out from the shadows, comforting them with the assurance that God can be trusted. In Wisdom we read the reason for trust: that God is "merciful to all, for you can do all things, and you overlook people's sins, so that they may repent. For you love all things that exist, and detest none of the things that you have made, for you would not have made anything if you had hated it. . . . You spare all things, for they are yours, O Lord, you who love the living."

As David Winston explains in his Anchor Bible commentary on this book,

Earlier in Wisdom we read that God could have crushed the Egyptians with one fell swoop if that was God's wish, [but] God . . . never acts arbitrarily, but always according to the laws of his own being. His omnipotence guarantees the unbiased character of his all-embracing love. The act of creation is itself a manifestation of this love, and precludes the possibility of divine hatred to any of his creatures. The deity therefore compassionately overlooks the sins of men with a constant view to their repentance. (*The Wisdom of Solomon: A New Translation with Introduction and Commentary*, The Anchor Bible, vol. 43 [New York: Doubleday, 1979], 231)

When Jesus looks at Zacchaeus, God incarnate does not see his sins, as numerous and major, or as few and petty, as they may be, but the person of Zacchaeus, a person scarred by life and his sins, as we all are to various degrees, but a person made in the image of God and loved by God. By climbing the tree, Zacchaeus has made it clear that he wants also to know God, to love God; the act of seeking Jesus out is itself an act of spiritual awareness and repentance.

The first thing Jesus tells Zacchaeus in Luke's account is that he wants to spend time with him: "Hurry and come down; for I must stay at your house today." Now that Zacchaeus is out from the shadows, Jesus' goal is not to scold him back into a dark corner, but to reveal to him the light. Zacchaeus "was happy to welcome him," but everyone else "began to grumble and said, 'He has gone to be the guest of one who is a sinner.'" This is true, but God could not dwell with anyone if God did not "overlook people's sins."

While human judgment can be harsh, God, who knows his creation through and through, accepts us as we are. By accepting Zacchaeus and his step toward him and inviting himself into his home, Jesus creates a relationship of intimacy, ignoring the petty grumbling of those who considered themselves more righteous than Zacchaeus. In this way, as the author of Wisdom says, "you correct little by little those who trespass, and you remind and warn them of the things through which they sin, so that they may be freed from wickedness and put their trust in you, O Lord." When Jesus puts his trust in Zacchaeus, overlooking his sins, Zacchaeus repents of his fraudulent past, offering to give half his possessions to the poor and to pay back fourfold those who were defrauded.

You cannot buy your salvation, but Zacchaeus' acts of contrition are signs of genuine repentance, so that Jesus can say, "Today salvation has come to this house." It has come indeed, for though the solution to sin seems counterintuitive—do not hide it, but confess it and bring it out into the open—it is a person, Jesus Christ, who was placed high on the cross for all to see, who, when you turn to him, cannot see your sins. They have been overlooked.

Visualize yourself in the crowd as Jesus calls out to Zacchaeus. How do you respond to Jesus' going to the house of Zacchaeus?

THE LIVING GOD

Thirty-Second Sunday in Ordinary Time

Readings: 2 Macc 7:1-14; Ps 17:1-15;
2 Thess 2:16–3:5; Luke 20:27-38

"Now he is God not of the dead, but of the living." (Luke 20:38)

As we ponder Jesus' confrontation with the Sadducees regarding life in the world to come, we are compelled to ask, "Do I believe in resurrection?" How one answers this question orients how we live today. It is a question that is not so much answered intellectually, though it is not beyond reason, as in the ordering of our loves. Who or what is our true love? Do we find our loves fulfilled in the living God or in the promises of this world?

To answer yes to resurrection is not a polemic against this world or our embodied nature, for the promise of resurrection of which Jesus speaks is not the denigration of our bodies or the rejection of our wholeness but the goal of our being. At some point we will all die; and that reality, and the hope of a future resurrection, does not diminish the importance of this life but makes it all the more significant.

The Sadducees, who answered no to resurrection, have tradition and, it seems, the Torah on their side. Apart from Daniel 12:1-4, little is said about resurrection in the Old Testament, especially the five books of the Torah. The Sadducees, a priestly, elite party, accepted the authority only of the Torah, and they did not find there any claims to resurrection. Indeed, what they found in the Torah was the law of levirate marriage, outlined in Deuteronomy 25:5-10. If a man died childless, his nearest male kin was to marry his widow, and the first child born to them was considered the child of the dead man, "so that his name may not be blotted out of Israel" (Deut 25:6).

The Sadducees propose to Jesus a ludicrous scenario as a means of demonstrating the foolishness of belief in resurrection. A woman was married to seven brothers, one after another, all of whom died childless.

"Finally the woman also died. In the resurrection, therefore, whose wife will the woman be? For the seven had married her." Jesus does not dismiss the question as foolish or reject it as a carefully designed trap, but uses it as an opportunity to teach.

First, Jesus says that marriage is about this world and the things of this world, not about the world to come, so the carefully crafted conundrum of the Sadducees is rejected. Second, Jesus draws on a passage from Exodus in which God says to Moses that he is "the God of Abraham, the God of Isaac, and the God of Jacob" (3:15). Jesus understands this as proof of the resurrection, for if God speaks of the current existence of Abraham, Isaac, and Jacob, this demonstrates that "he is God not of the dead, but of the living; for to him all of them are alive."

It is striking biblical interpretation, head-spinning really, for it suggests the untapped spiritual depth of a scriptural passage most of us would pass over as simply descriptive, but it was an essential proof for those who like the Sadducees rejected belief in the resurrection and accepted the scriptural authority of the Torah alone.

In fact, however, the majority of Jews in Jesus' day believed in resurrection, as had been the case since the Hellenistic period. Most groups, like the Pharisees, accepted resurrection, and many texts written in this period speak of it directly and often. But Jesus' interpretation grounds belief in resurrection not just in a Torah text the Sadducees would accept but, more important, in the nature of the living God as one who gives life to his creation and sustains that life beyond the limits of our understanding: the dead are never lost to God.

The belief and hope in the God of the living are seen in the seven Jewish martyrs of 2 Maccabees, all brothers, and in martyrs today, who offer their lives not out of a lust for suffering or as rejection of this world, but in trust of the living God. As the mother of the Maccabean martyrs says to them: "It was not I who gave you life and breath, nor I who set in order the elements within each of you. Therefore the Creator of the world, who shaped the beginning of humankind and devised the origin of all things, will in his mercy give life and breath back to you again" (2 Macc 7:22-23). This world and our choices matter, for it is the beginning of a life that God has ordered to go on forever.

Imagine yourself listening to Jesus with the Sadducees. Do you have a question for Jesus about the resurrection?

Life in the Balance

Readings: Mal 3:19-20; Ps 98:5-9;
2 Thess 3:7-12; Luke 21:5-19

"Teacher, when will this be?" (Luke 21:7)

There is an inherent tension in Christianity between the indicative and the imperative, what we are and what we are intended to be, between the present and the future, the life we are now living and the world to come. If we focus only on this world or only on the world to come, the Christian life is out of balance. For most of us, our attention is on the life we live now, but the *eschaton*, the end, the apocalypse is a part of the Christian hope and essential to keep in proper perspective and not ignore.

It can be easy to ignore out of lack of interest, lack of belief, weariness, or embarrassment. Some easily reject the mythic language of apocalyptic imagery. For others, the simple contrast between the righteous and the unrighteous, the one receiving an eternal reward, the other a fiery punishment, does not express their complex experience of life. And others have long tired of the cartoon representations of Christian apocalyptic thought found in popular American culture, in which pundits, politicians, and preachers vie with each other as to who can best interpret the last tornado, political change, or gun tragedy as the sign of the coming end.

But, to put it frankly, you cannot walk away from the end, however difficult it may be to translate it into a coherent vision of life in the twenty-first century. Why not? Jesus will not let you. Jesus speaks of the end in all three of the Synoptic Gospels and, in much less detail, in the Gospel of John, describing the apocalypse in language that is both chilling and confusing.

In Luke's gospel, Jesus says, "When you hear of wars and insurrections, do not be terrified; for these things must take place first, but the end will not follow immediately." Then he said to them, "Nation will rise against nation, and kingdom against kingdom; there will be great earthquakes, and in various places famines and plagues; and there will be dreadful portents and great signs from heaven." Events of this kind have been seen throughout history, though, and we are not to spend our time calculating the time of the end and interpreting portents.

The best balance is to concentrate on the reality that we will all face our end, whether the world ends in our lifetime or not, and to keep in mind that how we live in this life matters. No injustice, no cup of cold water given to one in need, is hidden from God who will bring all things to completion.

Malachi 3:17 uses straightforward language that sets apart the eschaton from every other day. There the voice of God speaks of "the day when I act." When we imagine the apocalyptic end apart from images of mythological forces of chaos and order, we must see the eschaton as the time when God will act decisively to bring about the perfect justice for which we all yearn.

In the midst of more revelations of alleged abuse of children in my archdiocese by people who have been my ministers and with whom I have worked, the crushing weight of sin seems to render perfect justice an illusion. The pain and loss of children who have been abused cries out to God to be vindicated. These allegations will find their way through court systems and tribunals, and human justice will be rendered, imperfectly and partially. But what will bind the brokenness, what will heal the wounds, what will render them whole?

Malachi directs us to this wholeness, saying, "The day is coming, burning like an oven, when all the arrogant and all evildoers will be stubble," but promising that "for you who revere my name the sun of righteousness shall rise, with healing in its wings."

Jesus promises that neither persecution nor betrayal by family or friends can turn one from God's righteousness; and this is true, too, for those who have been betrayed by ministers of the church. It is not vengeance that leads me to ache for "the day" when God acts; it is the desire to see justice rendered perfectly and to see those who have been disbelieved, dishonored, and dismissed rise with healing.

When will this be? The balanced answer is that the end begins now, and we respond by living justly and righteously, knowing that the end or our personal end could arrive at any time.

Reflect on the idea of the apocalypse. Do you see Judgment as hope and promise or condemnation?

THE True KING

The Solemnity of Christ the King

Readings: 2 Sam 5:1-3; Ps 122:1-5;
Col 1:12-20; Luke 23:35-43

"He is the image of the invisible God." (Col 1:15)

The whole nature of kingship can be confusing. At least it is confusing to me, raised as I was in Canada, a democracy that nevertheless retains a monarch as head of state. It does not necessarily get clearer in the United States, whose founding as an independent nation goes back to the casting off of an unjust king. These seem to be the two modern views of monarchs: pretty figureheads who wave to adoring crowds or petty tyrants who exploit their subjects. Neither model is particularly appealing and, more significant, neither model makes sense of the reality of Christ the King, the model of true kingship.

Confucius spoke of the need for the rectification of names in the political and social spheres, that unless people met the requirements of their name—like father, son, ruler, or subject—the society would be out of order. That is, one could be called a king, but if one did not embody the requirements of a true ruler, like benevolent treatment of subjects, one was not a true king but only a person who bore the name. From a Christian point of view, there have only been rulers who imperfectly bear the name of king, apart from Christ the King. The rectification of our understanding of kingship depends upon a proper understanding of the nature of Christ's kingship.

The people of Israel yearned for a king, and while the prophet Samuel warned them of the nature of every human king, God allowed them human kings. It was God who said of David, "It is you who shall be shepherd of my people Israel, you who shall be ruler over Israel." David did rule, for forty years, and in that time, apart from his great achievements, the Israelites could also reflect upon the adultery and murder committed by the great King David. He was a king like every other human king in so many respects. But God had also promised that his throne would be established forever. The Jews of the following centuries would await the fulfillment of the Davidic kingship, wondering, who would fulfill the messianic promises?

True kingship, it turns out, is a revelation. Having all power, Christ, the King of the universe, uses this power only to free us from the thrall of false kingdoms and kings, whether construed as human or spiritual kingship. The beautiful Christ hymn of Colossians, possibly a pre-Pauline hymn sung or recited in the earliest churches, tells us that God "rescued us from the power of darkness and transferred us into the kingdom of his beloved Son, in whom we have redemption, the forgiveness of sins." This kingdom, and Christ's kingship, was intended for subjects unworthy of the kingdom, in need of redemption from slavery but unable to foot the bill of the cost of freedom. Though "he is the image of the invisible God, the firstborn of all creation," and "all things have been created through him and for him," his task was to serve the cosmos and humanity through his role as suffering servant. In fact, "through him God was pleased to reconcile to himself all things, whether on earth or in heaven, by making peace through the blood of his cross."

The power of true kingship, it appears, is made manifest in this image: the King of the universe on the cross. We ought not to be surprised that the rulers, Luke tells us, "scoffed at him, saying, 'He saved others; let him save himself if he is the Messiah of God, his chosen one!'" or that "the soldiers also mocked him, coming up and offering him sour wine, and saying, 'If you are the King of the Jews, save yourself!'"

When the only kingship you know is the brute force of power to impose your will on others, it can be difficult to recognize that the true Ruler, the genuine King, acts not with arbitrary and malevolent force but with mercy. What a shock it must have been to the repentant criminal on the cross to realize that hanging beside him in his darkest hour was, in fact, God's beloved Son, who could transfer him from the power of darkness to God's kingdom. "Jesus, remember me when you come into your kingdom" is not so much a request as an acknowledgment: You are the true King!

Think of how Christ the King uses his power. How can you use the power you have in your day-to-day life to make more fully manifest God's kingdom?

Lightning Source UK Ltd.
Milton Keynes UK
UKHW02f2344250718
326292UK00006B/415/P